"Trust has never been more important in the corporate world—because there's so little of it. For years, people have tried to figure out how to communicate trust. Now, finally, Michael Maslansky has unlocked the DNA of trust. Anyone who cares about their employees, their customers, or their reputation has to read this book." **—Dr. Frank Luntz, author of *Words That Work* and *What Americans Really Want . . . Really***

"To successfully earn trust in face-to-face or Facebook communication, embrace the proven concepts in *The Language of Trust*—they're as important to your life as involuntary breathing. It's just common sense." **—Thomas L. Harrison, LHD, chairman and CEO of Diversified Agency Services division of Omnicom Group Inc.**

"Michael Maslansky has written the ultimate gui⁻ᵉ ᵗ g trust in a world that has lost it. He writes with ᵂⁱ dable absence of jargon. If you are concer⁻ , then this book is an indispensable startiₙ

 —Lord Go Prime Minister
To Communication

"Marketers, financial adviso ᵤₙᵢcators of all types should take note of the lessons in this book. The financial crisis has raised the bar for our industry. Now more than ever, the burden is on us to better understand our audience, and to use the right language and approaches if we are to even have a chance of connecting with them. *The Language of Trust* provides insightful and practical guidance that our industry would do well to follow. More than most, Michael understands the enormous challenges we face, and this book provides an essential set of tools and practical approaches for reconnecting with customers who may have lost faith in what we offer. It isn't enough for us to have a good story to tell; we must also be able to tell a good—and credible—story. *The Language of Trust* will help any communicator who must win over a skeptical audience." **—Cathy Weatherford, CEO of Insured Retirement Institute**

"Today's polarized discourse makes it hard to understand problems, much less fix them. *The Language of Trust* provides the core principles needed for moving forward." **—Philip K. Howard, founder of Common Good and author of *The Death of Common Sense* and *Life Without Lawyers***

"There are many books on effective communication, but this book is unique in the way it recognizes the importance of language and messaging as ways to build trust when talking to customers, partners, or employees. *The Language of Trust* will help any executive who must communicate with strength and credibility." **—Suzanne Coulter, president of Polo Retail Corporation**

The
Language of
TRUST

Selling Ideas in a World of Skeptics

Michael Maslansky
with Scott West, Gary DeMoss, and David Saylor

PRENTICE HALL PRESS

PRENTICE HALL PRESS
Published by the Penguin Group
Penguin Group (USA) Inc.
375 Hudson Street, New York, New York 10014, USA
Penguin Group (Canada), 90 Eglinton Avenue East, Suite 700, Toronto, Ontario M4P 2Y3, Canada
(a division of Pearson Penguin Canada Inc.)
Penguin Books Ltd., 80 Strand, London WC2R 0RL, England
Penguin Group Ireland, 25 St. Stephen's Green, Dublin 2, Ireland (a division of Penguin Books Ltd.)
Penguin Group (Australia), 250 Camberwell Road, Camberwell, Victoria 3124, Australia
(a division of Pearson Australia Group Pty. Ltd.)
Penguin Books India Pvt. Ltd., 11 Community Centre, Panchsheel Park, New Delhi—110 017, India
Penguin Group (NZ), 67 Apollo Drive, Rosedale, North Shore 0632, New Zealand
(a division of Pearson New Zealand Ltd.)
Penguin Books (South Africa) (Pty.) Ltd., 24 Sturdee Avenue, Rosebank, Johannesburg 2196,
South Africa

Penguin Books Ltd., Registered Offices: 80 Strand, London WC2R 0RL, England

While the author has made every effort to provide accurate telephone numbers and Internet addresses at the time of publication, neither the publisher nor the author assumes any responsibility for errors, or for changes that occur after publication. Further, the publisher does not have any control over and does not assume any responsibility for author or third-party websites or their content.

PRINTING HISTORY
Prentice Hall Press hardcover edition / May 2010
Prentice Hall Press trade paperback edition / May 2011

Prentice Hall Press trade paperback ISBN: 978-0-7352-0456-0

The Library of Congress had cataloged the Prentice Hall Press hardcover edition as follows:

The language of trust : selling ideas in a world of skeptics / Michael Maslansky . . . [et al.].— 1st ed.
    p. cm.
Includes bibliographical references and index.
ISBN 978-0-7352-0475-1
1. Business communication. 2. Trust. 3. Interpersonal communication. 4. Customer
relations. I. Maslansky, Michael.
HF5718.L369 2010
    658.4'5—dc22   2009053933

PRINTED IN THE UNITED STATES OF AMERICA

10   9   8

Most Prentice Hall Press books are available at special quantity discounts for bulk purchases for sales promotions, premiums, fund-raising, or educational use. Special books, or book excerpts, can also be created to fit specific needs. For details, write: Special Markets, Penguin Group (USA) Inc., 375 Hudson Street, New York, New York 10014.

Contents

Acknowledgments

For ideation and creation, thanks to Gary, Scott, and Dave, and my colleague Lee Carter, for starting us down the New Word Order path that led to this book.

For narration, elucidation, and a fair bit of perspiration, thanks to Mike Phifer and Jennifer Gilbert, who were irreplaceable in creating a work of which we can be proud.

For dedication and consultation, thanks to my whole team at Maslansky, Luntz & Partners for doing the work that underpins this book and for keeping us going in good times and, well, less good times.

For challenging situations, high expectations, and sustaining my vocation, thanks to my great clients (and even my not so great ones), who have provided an incredible diversity of issues, brands, and products that make my job interesting every day.

For education and exhortation, thanks to Frank Luntz for introducing me to the world of language and showing how powerful it can be.

For publication and public relations, thanks to our editors John Duff and Maria Gagliano, literary agent Diana Finch, and the team at Prentice Hall Press and Penguin.

And for inspiration and motivation, but never aggravation, love to Susie, Morgan, and Max.

Welcome to the
World of Skeptics

Close your eyes. Okay, just figuratively. Now imagine for a moment a world where everyone believes you. Imagine not needing to hire PR agencies and crisis management communication teams because when bad things happen, you can just go out there and provide a reasonable explanation . . . and people believe you. Imagine being able to sell your widget without being peppered with objections and questions and information gleaned by your prospect from negative product reviews or outspoken critics. Imagine a world where you are given the benefit of the doubt that what you say is true. Where no one is skeptical.

Okay, now wake up.

It might be fun to imagine a world where skepticism is fantasy and trust just happens, but it doesn't do us any good. Just about anyone in the business of selling ideas—be they products, brands, issues, or ourselves—gets up and goes to work with the feeling that half the people we need to convince don't trust us, and the other half don't even want to hear what we have to say. When our intentions are good, we are doubted. When our products are good, people assume there is a catch. When we tell a positive story, people assume we are hiding something. And if we happen to work for a large corporation, people assume that we are out to profit at their expense. There is no benefit of the doubt, only a higher degree of skepticism than ever before.

Simply put, trust is dead.

This is a big statement, but I believe it is the fundamental reason why our public discourse, our corporate communication, and our traditional sales techniques have pretty much fallen off a cliff. I can't find an exact moment when this all happened because there isn't an exact moment. Over the years, with the weight of our accumulated experiences, we've simply become more distrustful of everyone and everything around us. We don't trust the government to look out for us. We don't trust companies to do right by us. We don't trust each other to take responsibility for ourselves anymore. And we don't even trust our own families to be there for us. Of course there are exceptions to all of these statements, but the general trend is undeniable: trust in America—and around the world—is headed for the dustbin. We now live in an era of mistrust.

For better or worse, consumers now view companies and salespeople much like the prototypical used-car salesman. Whether we are talking about our products, our corporate social responsibility, or our position on important policy issues, most people assume that we have an ulterior motive—that we are putting our own interests in front of theirs; that we are overpromising and underdelivering; or that we are cherry-picking statistics to prove our point.

Increasingly, the critics—from the news media to bloggers to past customers—are reinforcing these negative assessments with more force (and a louder voice) than you and your allies can combat. Consumers don't trust you, so they are finding their own facts.

They are seeking others' opinions. They are looking to peers—real and virtual—to get their view of your product or position. This age of mistrust is unlike any other because it's so easy for consumers to confirm their skepticism. Our digital echo chamber of twenty-four-hour cable news and Internet everywhere, all the time, has made our job as communicators harder than ever.

I'm a language guy, so it shouldn't be any surprise when I say that language is a big contributor to this decline in trust and rise in skepticism—and it can also be a big part of the solution. Human communication, since the beginning of its existence, has always been a sort of trial and error game. There are no universal, fundamental rules that govern language the way there are rules that govern mathematics, physics, chemistry, and the other "hard sciences."

Language is an art. It's an art we all practice, all the time, but it's an art nonetheless. We create rules of syntax and grammar so that language is efficient, manageable, and meaningful. But these rules can vary widely from one language to the next (English speakers say "blue car," whereas the French say "car blue") because we are the ones who give them meaning.

As a result, language gets manipulated. People play with language, see how it affects others based on their reactions, and then use language to their advantage. Unlike many forms of art, language is also an extremely useful tool in our daily lives—one that humans have used (and misused) since our knuckles finally came off the ground.

The fact that language has been a tool used to manipulate people for quite a long time is no small point. Throughout history, language has been used to enslave, conquer, oppress, and even exterminate people because it is so powerful. On the flip side, language (often followed up by overwhelming force) has also been used to remedy or undo those same awful things. Plato, someone who knew a thing or two about language, said: "Rhetoric is the art of ruling the minds of men." The problem with rhetoric in this sense is that its misuse has, quite frankly, come back to bite us in the ass.

In the twenty-first century, rhetoric is known as "spin." There are entire industries set up to worship at the altar of spin, and regardless of the person in office at the time, 1600 Pennsylvania Avenue is its holy cathedral. What this book is *not* about is spin.

Using language to create effective and credible communication is not spin. Using one word or phrase instead of another to explain the same idea is not spin. Creating a process of storytelling about your idea or product that makes people interested is not spin. Putting facts, figures, and arguments in context for your audience is not spin. Understanding who your audience is and speaking directly to them is not spin. Saying "it depends on what the meaning of the word 'is' is"[1] is not spin.

Well, okay, maybe that last one is spin. But you get the idea.

This book is not about how to spin messages to fool people. No amount of linguistic massaging is going to turn a bad company into a good one or make something done with malicious intent into something positive. Yes, these approaches can be used to try to put lipstick on the proverbial pig. And yes, you can fool a lot of the people a lot of the time. But to build trust, words must align with actions. Language without supportive behavior does not create lasting trust; it creates a stronger foundation for skepticism.

This book is about how to use language to undo the skepticism that a world of too much spin has created. This book is for situations where you have something worth listening to but can't get the message through. It focuses on giving you the tools to use language to build, or rebuild, trust when the facts, actions, and record are on your side, but you just can't quite get over that last hurdle—acceptance.

Who Is This Book For?

This profound skepticism running rampant is not some esoteric concept. It affects a surprising number of conversations we have in our personal and professional lives. We are skeptical about the salesperson who says that their product is better than the competition. We are skeptical of the customer who says that they "just want to think about it" and will be back to you shortly. We are skeptical of the manager who tells us that our job is secure and that we have a future inside the organization. And we are skeptical of the job seeker who tries to explain why they are the perfect fit for the organization. We are skeptical of the company that says it cares about its customers or that it is committed to the environment. We are skeptical of CEOs and politicians and the promises they make. We are also skeptical of the blogger who attacks those CEOs and politicians. We are skeptical of the professional product reviewers because they may be in the pockets of companies. And we are skeptical of the random user review because we have no idea who this person is or why that person should be trusted. And when faced with even a single piece of information that raises doubt, we often become skeptical in our personal relationships.

And once this skepticism exists, it is extremely difficult to overcome. The right actions help. But if the skeptic has turned you off or tuned you out, then these actions will go unnoticed and unappreciated.

My hope is that this book will be of interest to anyone who

finds himself in a situation where the message you are trying to send matters. You may find examples that are directly relevant to your industry or situation. You may not. What we have learned over the course of time is that humans are, well, consistently human. People's skepticism is remarkably consistent across audiences, issues, and industries, as are the ways that they react to different communication approaches. Based on research I have conducted in local languages in almost thirty countries, I can also say that it is consistent from market to market. Skepticism varies from the most skeptical in the UK to the most accepting in developing countries like India, and opinions diverge wildly on everything from the environment to advertising to the stock market. But the approaches needed to engage the public and build trust are remarkably consistent. I hope you will find lessons that you can apply directly to your specific situation and that you finish this book with a broadened perspective and some new ideas about how to put these principles into action.

This book is for anyone who must navigate this sea of skepticism to sell ideas, products, services, and even themselves to a public that just doesn't want to hear it.

It is for:

- Corporate communicators who have to connect with the public about controversial topics or clean up the PR mess from a corporate scandal or other exigent situation.

- Salespeople who want to better understand what their customers may be thinking, and how to better connect with them.

- Managers seeking to build employee trust and morale or motivate and engage their employees.

- Marketers who want to achieve better sales results for their products (except if you work at a place like Apple, in which case the product does a great job of selling itself!).

- Employees and job seekers who must constantly sell themselves and their achievements to people they want to impress.

For some of you, we will challenge a lifetime of speaking habits. We will explore words to use, words to lose, and a new order for structuring your message. Above all we will give you real-world examples, ranging from politics to finance, that show how real people now react to what you say and how you say it. By learning how to communicate with a new language in an era of mistrust, you can fundamentally change the relationship between you and those you seek to convince, sway, or upsell.

That's what the language of trust is all about.

An Approach Built on Research

This book has its roots in a unique combination of quantitative and qualitative research that reveals social trends and psychological dispositions. It is also based on thousands of Instant Response sessions (explained later), focus groups, and surveys that reveal an amazing consistency in the way we as humans respond to messaging and communication—almost regardless of issue or geography.

My firm specializes in studying the impact of the words we use and how to employ them more effectively. Our testing is based on emotional—rather than rational—responses to messaging because we see time and again that people respond to messages with their heart before they do with their brain. We have conducted research in nearly every major industry—from health care to energy, technology to food and beverage, from real estate development to personal care products. We have also conducted research across an incredible range of topics to understand how people react to changes in taxation, regulation, and reputational issues. In every case, we test different messages with audiences to identify what works, what doesn't, and why. And because so much of our research points to the importance of building trust as the critical first step in selling any idea, I have brought our lessons learned together in this book.

Don't Touch That Dial

If you have ever watched coverage of a major presidential debate on cable news networks such as CNN, you have seen one of the key instruments of our research: an audience of people registering their reactions in real time using individual dials that are in each person's hand.

These devices are generally calibrated on a scale from 0 to 100, ranging from a completely negative reaction to a completely positive one. Participants are instructed to set their dials at 50 (representing a neutral reaction), and then to "dial up" or "dial down" based on how they react to what they are hearing. The scores of the group are then aggregated, and a line representing the average is often displayed on a video screen in real time to viewers along with the message being tested.

We use this approach to test messages because it tests the emotional, instantaneous response to messages. Before the viewer knows why they like or dislike a message, they can register their reaction, telling us what their heart feels before we listen to what their head thinks. Another important aspect of what we call Instant Response testing is that it allows us to break down the results by demographics. During a political debate, for example, it is not unusual to see different-colored lines representing each party affiliation, or men versus women, or both.

These lines represent trends that combine individual anonymity with the overall mind-set of an entire group.

Dial testing results are not shown to the participants themselves in real time, to avoid having the group's reactions influence those of each other. But we often show them to live audiences by projecting them behind these participants on stage, giving people a rare view of that "thought bubble" of what's in the participants' minds. More important, these data become part of a wider evidence base that teaches us how people react to what we say.

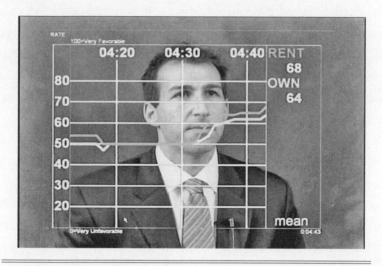

I have the privilege of working with a group of coauthors who work on the front lines with today's consumers. They work in an industry that depends more on building trust and credibility than perhaps any other—financial services. They work with people who ask every day to become stewards of their clients' life savings and so they have a unique perspective on the importance of building trust and the techniques that have worked—or failed—with thousands of these financial advisors. Though this book is not specifically about financial communications, many of the examples in this book relate to work that we have done in the variable annuities industry. In fact, this book emanated in part from our collaborative research in this area. We didn't pick this focus because it is inherently interesting to many of the people we hope will read this book. We picked it because variable annuities suffer from some of the most challenging circumstances that salespeople and corporate communicators face on a regular basis.

We also picked it because it is a great example of a product that must sell on its own merits. It is fairly easy to sell an iPhone. Hell, they practically sell themselves. But try selling a product that 76 percent of the population says they don't know about, don't care about, or don't like. Like many of the products and issues on which we work, variable annuities suffer from a major credibility problem. They are misunderstood, overly complex products with a history of negative baggage. It's hard to sell them. Combine that with the fact that they are the subject of constant attacks from financial analysts in the media, and it's almost impossible. And yet investors own nearly one and a half trillion dollars worth of them in the United States today.[2]

Ultimately, this book is about understanding people. I know there have been enough books written on the subject to fill several large, mahogany-paneled rooms, but I haven't found one that focuses on language—the specific words, phrases, and approaches to communicating—quite the way we do. I've spent years and thousands of hours watching and listening to people as they react to messages across an incredible range of topics, asking them why they feel and react the way they do, and trying to understand how language—from simple words to complex arguments—affects their perceptions of business, government, and even their next-door neighbors. This book is a distillation of those experiences.

Why Should You Trust a Book About Trust?

The only books I know of that stand the chance of changing your life are history's great works—the ones that revolutionize the way we think, the way we act, and the way we understand the human experience. Admittedly, this one will not evoke such a transformative experience. Nor will it necessarily transform the way you solve every communication problem you face today or in the future.

What it will do is provide a set of straightforward principles based on the latest cultural and communication research that shed light on a very modern problem: how to communicate in a credible and impactful way at a time when credibility is in extremely short supply.

One thing you should know and remember is that this book is not simply a collection of my own opinions and musings on the subject. Instead, it represents the accumulated feedback from quantitative and qualitative research with voters, consumers, members of the media, employees, shareholders, and even congressional staffers about how to communicate in ways that overcome their skepticism and effectively present new ideas or products. These audiences have no agenda (in this context, at least) other than to share their thoughts. As a result, their reactions and opinions provide some amazing insight into why some of the most deeply held approaches to professional communication are out and out wrong.

Some people question books of principles because principles are so easily refuted. I agree. Effective communication is highly contextual, and no set of guidelines will work in all situations at all times. We reject negative messages in this book, but recognize that, at times, negative messages do indeed work, polarizing language is effective, and extreme promises sway people. But these are exceptions and not the rule. What we have found time and time again is that, when faced with a skeptical audience who you need to reach—to buy your product, vote for you, or support your agenda, whatever it is—the language of trust will help you succeed.

Others may question this book in particular as coming from the CEO of a company founded by Frank Luntz, the famous—or in some circles infamous—pollster and "spin doctor." This too is a valid question. It's a fact that effective, impactful communication tactics can help people promote ideas across the political—and moral—spectrum, no matter how valid or not we find them. Which is exactly why communicators of all stripes who are struggling to get their message across to skeptical audiences will be well served by reading this book. In the end, your audience will be the final arbiters of what you have to say. But only if you succeed in reaching them in a way they find believable.

PART ONE

THE NEW LANGUAGE OF TRUST

I don't believe it. Prove it to me and I still won't believe it.

—Douglas Adams, author of
Hitchhiker's Guide to the Galaxy

This is the world we live in today. It is not limited to any one industry or issue or company. Nor is it limited by geography. I have faced skeptics in Japan on financial services, China on the environment, Western Europe on alternative energy, and Brazil on health and wellness. In every place and every issue, the challenge is the same: when skepticism is the rule, how do you overcome the doubt to get someone to believe?

To many communicators the challenge is a rational one; simply a question of marshaling the right facts and arguments. It is these people who often get most frustrated when they can't get their message through. In my experience, overcoming skepticism is much more about emotion than it is about rationality. People must want to believe you before they will believe you. Much of the job of effective communication is about building that foundation of openness so that a message can be accepted.

The language of trust is based on a belief that your communication can change people's minds about an issue or product but rarely can you change that person's view of the world. Sales conversations are too short. Political communication is too often restricted to sound bites and talking points. And most people naturally filter out messages that do not conform to what they already believe. So rather than confronting them at the level of their core, we look for approaches that allow them to buy what we are selling without compromising those core beliefs. In other words, we want to find the areas of alignment between our idea and their worldview.

Communicating in this way requires an understanding of how skeptics think as well as the key factors driving their increased skepticism. In other words, to convince skeptics, we must first learn how they view the world and accept their view as valid. From that position we can then engage them and persuade them to listen to what we have to say. Chapter 1 explores the roots of mistrust and the factors that are contributing to a rapid rise in skepticism in our society. This chapter also covers what this increased skepticism means for how we operate and why losing the benefit of the doubt has real financial consequences for organizations of all types. Finally, Chapter 1 talks about how the loss of trust has turned many of the traditional approaches to communication on their head.

Chapter 2 then lays out the framework for the language of trust: what it is and how you can apply it to a range of common business situations. I will talk about how this language differs from other approaches to sales and issue communications. And in this chapter, I also outline the four principles of credible communication—the tools you need to build messages that overcome skepticism and build trust.

1

America's Post-Trust Era

RIP
Americans' Trust in America
1776–2008

Imagine, for a moment, an America where a controversial foreign war has been dragging on for five years, costing countless billions of dollars and thousands of American lives.

Imagine an America where half the people distrust and resent the current president, and the other half distrust and resent the charismatic young man destined to replace him.

Imagine corporate CEOs so detached from reality they take private jets to congressional hearings to grovel for taxpayer bailouts.

Imagine the world's biggest and most trusted banks and investment firms casually and irresponsibly gambling away people's entire life savings in pursuit of their next quarterly bonuses.

Imagine some of the most trusted political, business, economic, and community leaders in this country exposed as incompetent or, worse, cheats and liars.

And while this country has gone through wars, economic meltdowns, and crises of confidence in the past, imagine all of this occurring amid an environment that has in many ways abandoned the very means people would traditionally use to understand and process what's going on, amid a media landscape transformed over the past twenty years by a thousandfold explosion of channels, voices, and opinions and the proliferation of the Internet and blogosphere, amid a radically new reality in which the cultural authority and moderating force of the traditional mass media have been replaced by a self-service, do-it-yourself system in which people are on their own to seek out information and judge its credibility.

Welcome to 2008, the year trust finally died in America.

Yes, that's a bold statement. But based on years of research and hundreds of conversations with leaders of Fortune 500 companies and mid-caps, politicians and political operatives, nonprofit organizations and charities, 2008 was when the decades-long erosion of trust in this country's institutions finally reached the breaking point.

For communicators, the consequences are clear. Whether you're a food and beverage company talking about your products' nutrition, an energy company talking about your green initiatives, or a mortgage company trying to reconnect with frustrated home owners, the bar for credible communications has been raised to the ceiling. Voters, customers, and even employees look at institutions differently now than in decades past. They challenge your credibility before even listening to what you have to say. They look first for exceptions and contradictions instead of reasons to believe. They assume from the beginning that institutions and people have bad motives. And as a result, the same old approaches to getting your message across simply don't work. No matter the industry, no matter the subject, no matter the challenge, this marked shift in America's level of trust has reshaped the way we must think about communicating at every level.

Every year, public relations firm Edelman tracks people's level of trust in everything from their news outlets to their banks. The 2009 Trust Barometer found that three out of four Americans trust business less than a year ago. To make things worse, trust levels are down in every major market segment.

And instead of at least trusting the fourth estate—the media—to help us sort truth from fiction, the Trust Barometer shows that people trust the news media even less than they do business and government. The most popular cable TV news outlets are split along party lines, letting viewers choose the truth they want to hear. People can't agree about the very facts that underlie the major debates of our age.

In short, this is not a blip on the screen. This is a transformation in trust. And for anyone with anything important to communicate to people, it's a crisis different than any we have seen before. So what are we to do?

The Roots of Mistrust

Just a few years ago, salespeople, corporate leaders, marketing departments, and communicators like me had it pretty easy. We looked at communication as a relatively linear process. We used to tell clients to sell emotional benefits. Create the vision. Contrast the alternatives. Be aspirational—remind people of patriotism, apple pie, the American Dream, and kittens. Those were the golden days of boilerplate communication . . . and we could sell you almost anything. That was an America where companies were able to tell their story and be heard. We hadn't seen real economic crisis in decades, and Pepsi's so-called Generation Next was riding the wave of unprecedented growth and prosperity. But trust disappeared, things changed. We are now communicating in the post-trust era (PTE).

Yesterday's trust has become today's skepticism. The simple path doesn't work anymore. You communicate simple truths about your product and no one believes you. You create vision statements and hang banners on the walls of your company, but your turnover is still off the charts. And politicians' approval ratings are among the lowest in history.

In the 2010 PTE, people are more sensitive than ever to manipulation by communication. In our research, people dismiss ads and other communication for not passing "the smell test." They respond to straightforward facts by saying that statistics can be manipulated to support any story. They assume that companies are purposely leaving out important information.

Whether you're selling an idea, a candidate, a widget, or yourself, "just trust me" just isn't enough. In fact, the more you try to convey that you're better, safer, or smarter than the competition, the less likely people are to believe you.

In a phrase, trust is out, skepticism is in.

A skeptic is someone who challenges ideas in search of the truth. In practice, skepticism involves taking the time to better understand and therefore make the best decision. This is perfectly healthy. When asked, most people claim the opposite of skepticism to be optimism. Not true. It is actually gullibility. An optimist knows everything will be good. A cynic knows that everything will be bad. Someone who is gullible believes without questioning. A skeptic gathers more information. Typically people generally become more skeptical as they gather more experience in the world, but today skepticism is found everywhere, from the young to the old. Here are some of the reasons why:

We have much more information. Once upon a time, people claimed to have the best product, and we believed them. People could stand on soapboxes in the public square and sell snake oil to the masses. They frightened us into buying their wares . . . or else. Those tactics worked, for the most part, because the average Joe simply didn't know any better, and certainly didn't have Google to help him make the right decisions. Before we make purchases now, we check consumer ratings on Amazon.com, peruse reviews on Epinions.com, and we scan the blogs for negative feedback or firsthand accounts. We are connected as a digital community, share our opinions at light speed, and can verify the truth of messages we hear faster than ever before.

We have seen behind the curtain. More than ever before, the art and science of marketing and communications are part of pop culture. In political communications, there is as much debate about how messages are used to sell policy as there is about the policies themselves. At the same time, we see voracious competition among marketers looking to use the slightest—often meaningless—edge in their marketing to gain a competitive advantage. Over time we have gained extensive experience deconstructing communication. And we have become more sophisticated consumers as a result.

We don't want to be told what to think. If you are a parent, you have certainly learned that the quickest way to get your children to say no to something is to tell them that it is good for them. In many ways, we as consumers have all become children and the companies and institutions trying to communicate with us are the parents. We reject their suggestions simply because it comes from them. As a result, the most credible and effective sales pitches today are often not sales pitches at all. They give information, not hype, and put control in the hands of the consumer.

We have shorter attention spans. Decades ago, it wasn't unusual for ads on television to be two minutes long and insurance salespeople to visit us in person. Now we barely glance at a banner ad as we buy the same insurance over the Internet. Most of us now live in a 24/7, two hundred–plus channel, always connected, online world where countless things constantly compete for our attention—and our dollars. Millions of people now routinely communicate in 140 characters or less via sites like Twitter and Facebook. We reduced phone conversations to messages, messages to texts, texts to symbols. If we're happy, you will not hear it or read it. You'll see it. :) Thanks to these seemingly miraculous, if not often annoying advancements, modern communicators not only have a higher burden of credibility, but less time to build it.

Stir all of these things together with factors ranging from more information to more complex products, and you have the new, digitally fueled age of the skeptic. You have America in the PTE.

It's the Symbols, Stupid

Another sign of the erosion of trust in American life is how symbols have increasingly come to dominate public discourse.

Multimillion-dollar compensation packages. Private jets. Hormones in milk. Plastic water bottles. Chemicals in baby products. High credit card rates. Lavish bonuses on Wall Street.

What do these things have in common? At first, it might seem like nothing. But when you take a step back and think about the context in which things like these are usually discussed, their similarities become apparent. Each is a symbol—a shorthand representation of a much larger ideological perspective. And each poses a specific challenge to a company or industry without saying a word.

The Symbol	What It Says
Multimillion-dollar compensation packages	Rewards for bad behavior.
Private jets	Protection of the privileged.
Hormones in milk	The food we feed our families is no longer pure.
Plastic water bottles	Environmental scourge.
Chemicals in baby products	Anything to make a buck.
High credit card rates	We will take advantage of you at every turn.
Retention bonuses on Wall Street	The ultimate hypocrisy.
Steroids in baseball	The rules don't apply to us.

While symbolism has played an important role for millennia, in the PTE, symbols dominate the debate in American public life. Put yourself in the shoes of Rick Wagoner, former CEO of GM, as he tries to tell Congress about why his company needs a government bailout on the same day he and other executives flew separate private jets from Detroit to Washington. He might have the best reasons and the most compelling argument to justify public support. But in the eyes of the public, the symbol of the private jet completely overshadowed his plea for a bailout.

CEO compensation is another powerful recent symbol. At most major companies, executive compensation represents a tiny fraction of the overall expenses that contribute to a product's cost. Eliminating all senior executive salaries at your average public company would have virtually zero impact on the cost of its products. But CEO compensation is a symbol—it reflects the broadly held perception that companies enrich themselves at the expense of their customers. So, in industry after industry, it becomes extremely difficult to have a conversation about the positive things a company is doing as long as those symbols dominate the consumers' perceptions.

The media compound the problem as outlets compete for viewers and readership by telling the simplest, starkest stories and basing them on symbols that are easily digestible and difficult to refute. Complex subjects are reduced to taglines, nuance is lost, and the opportunities for real, engaged discussion disappear.

To make things worse, public avenues for symbol-driven communication are so viral and instantaneous that these symbols have increasing power to drive public opinion, drive legislative action, and dramatically impact the way companies do business. By the time a traditional newspaper has gone to press, social media and blogs can spread a set of resonant symbols around the planet, often complete with streaming video.

#Amazonfail

In April 2009, a large number of books relating to gay themes lost their Amazon.com sales rank, causing them to also lose visibility in Amazon .com's search and listing pages. Almost immediately, there was an uproar on Twitter under the hashtag (or keyword) #amazonfail. The overwhelming conclusion was that Amazon.com had acted intentionally, and inappropriately, to discriminate against a group discriminated against in the past. No one went to get the facts. No one gave Amazon.com time to explain up front. Instead, thousands, if not tens of thousands, of people on Twitter, came to the conclusion that Amazon.com was a bad company because the symbolism of these titles losing their rank was too strong to ignore.

The reality was that it was a technological glitch. And while Amazon .com likely deserves some culpability for their handling of the whole incident, the lesson is clear. As one blogger wrote: "The idea that this was an event of mainly technological propagation, rather than a coordinated bit of . . . bias, simply escaped me. This isn't because I am a generally stupid person; it was because I was, on [that day], a specifically stupid person. When a lifetime of intellectual labor and study came up against a moment of emotional engagement, emotion won, in a rout."[3]

The Impact of Skepticism on How We Operate

While the fallout from the implosion of trust has yet to fully settle, everyone from politicians to a person arguing in favor of organic milk through their Facebook page realizes just how difficult it is to sell ideas in the PTE. And even as we begin this relatively young era, it's clear that big business—never having occupied a soft spot in the American heart—has a particularly daunting task ahead of it. No longer just the target of fringe elements and the vocal minority, corporations are increasingly cast as the primary villain.

While I would never base a client's analysis on a review of what's playing at the local cineplex, it's telling that corporations and their CEOs (almost always old, white, and permanently grimacing) are brought to justice at the conclusion of many of today's feature films at a notable rate.

This phenomenon hasn't happened overnight, but you can clearly track the evolution of villainy in American film from bank robbers to spies to CEOs. From Michael Moore's *Roger and Me* to *Erin Brockovich* to the remake of *The Manchurian Candidate*, big business is increasingly the bad guy pulling the strings. Even children's movies have taken up the cause. In *Wall-E*, a large corporation basically took over the world and polluted it beyond repair, while in *Happy Feet*, the penguin food supply was depleted by greedy, uncaring corporate fishermen. Poor penguins, they never catch a break. They can't even fly.

The point of all this is that the impact of mistrust and the power of negative symbols is becoming more and more evident in the PTE. Art is imitating life and increasingly reflects the growing disdain for corporations among average, everyday Americans. Not only do people mistrust companies, but the popular culture is actively turning them into boogeymen. Even scarier is the fact that this newfound mistrust doesn't stop with Fortune 500 companies trying to make a profit. Communicators of all stripes are finding it harder and harder to get their messages across, regardless of how factual or well intentioned they are, precisely because trust in anything "big" is withering on the vine.

I have worked with philanthropies with tremendous credentials that face the same level of skepticism as the largest corporations. I have seen employees turn from committed participants in a corporate mission to jaded, skeptical naysayers in a matter of months. Large company and small, political and corporate, for profit and not-for-profit, the challenges are the same. If you're trying to sell something—widgets, ideas, candidates, anything—you face an uphill battle from the start because, quite frankly, people just don't believe you, especially if you're the one in charge.

The impact of this shift in attitude is not just a question for parlor conversation. The effects of this mistrust are far-reaching and impact everything from our buying decisions to our personal finances.

More and more consumers are making purchasing decisions based on more than the product or service. They are looking at the overall reputation of the company—how it operates, treats its employees, the environment and the communities in which it operates—and deciding whether or not they want to do business with that company. According to the Edelman survey on trust, 77 percent of people surveyed refused to purchase a product or service because they did not trust the company behind it. Wal-Mart is a great example. Despite the fact that Wal-Mart is almost always the best place to get a given product for the lowest price, we consistently heard in focus groups around the country that a small but significant population would drive by the local Wal-Mart to pay more someplace else. Why? The lasting impact of news stories that Wal-Mart mistreated its employees shattered trust in the company for these people. And their choice was to spend more and drive farther rather than shop at Wal-Mart.

The reality—and this is a hard one for many marketers to deal with—is that it is no longer enough to just sell your product. Pharmaceutical companies cannot simply focus on marketing their latest medication. Insurance companies can no longer just sell the coverage they offer. And even bottled water companies can't sell something as simple and pure as bottled water. In every case listed, and in virtually every other category as well, the lack of trust in companies to be good companies means that marketers need to spend an increasing amount of their time and their voice selling things that were never traditionally part of the marketing discussion.

Put simply, marketers are now being forced to divert precious resources away from marketing their product benefits and to trying to overcome reputation risks. Though this battle for reputation on things like the environment and health and wellness does create competitive opportunities, many marketers see it as a painful price to pay to deal with the realities of a skeptical world.

Companies have become easier targets for legislation, regulation, and taxation. Other than lobbyists, fewer and fewer people are willing to stand up and defend corporate America. And for a country built on the American Dream and the idolization of iconic CEOs of the past, that is a significant fall from grace. As one CEO told me recently, "Despite all the good things we do and are trying to do, I walk around feeling like I have a bull's eye on my back." When trust is missing, the defenses against an onslaught of attacks are much weaker.

For many, altruism is also dead. Even benevolent, well-intentioned actions can run into a brick wall of skepticism. Doing the right thing is no longer enough. Today, credibility requires that you must also communicate whatever you're doing the right way because ulterior motives are now considered the rule, not the exception.

Recently, we conducted 401(k) research to explore what employers could do for their employees to encourage them to save more for retirement—surely a noble goal by any reasonable account. Experts across the board have suggested that 7 percent of salary is a good starting point for retirement savings. With that in mind, we asked people how they would feel if "your employer set an *automatic* 401(k) contribution rate of 7 percent of your salary, but gave you the option to change the rate if you wanted to." More than half of the people we asked rejected this approach because they felt it was an example of an employer inappropriately interfering with employees' take-home pay or, worse, a scheme to benefit the employer. In reality, the company's decision to actively promote more savings was designed to help address the fact that forced savings has been shown to be one of the only ways to get people to save for their future. Despite this altruistic goal, the company's efforts were rejected because of lack of trust.

This is where the language of trust starts to change everything about the relationship between you and your audience. When we took this hypothetical situation of deducting 7 percent for retirement, and changed the way it was communicated, the results were dramatic.

Using Language to Build Trust

Compare these four sets of statements:

1. "This process is automatic, but not required. It's voluntary. If you don't want to be enrolled or you don't like any of the choices we made, you can always opt-down to a lower level or opt-out."

2. "We have established the investment rate and default option based on general retirement guidelines, but you may change your investment rate or stop participating in the plan at any time."

3. "We do not want to tell you what to do with your money, but we do want to help you understand your options and make the most of the money that you do save for retirement."

4. "We believe we have a responsibility to provide you with information and guidance about the most effective strategies for saving and investing to achieve your retirement goals."

All sound reasonable on the surface. But while the first statement resonates with 40 percent of the population, the second and third resonate with less than a quarter, and the last resonates with only 15 percent. *But they all say exactly the same thing.*

Look again at the statements. The fourth statement represents what many companies believe. In my experience, the overwhelming majority of HR leaders and senior executives do care about their employees. They may or may not have personal relationships, but they certainly have vested professional interests in helping employees to succeed inside and outside the workplace. The problem we identified here—and have seen in project after project—is that employees reject this notion.

It simply isn't credible. So, to do a good thing, the smart company will change their approach. Rather than trying to communicate their intent, they will go out of their way to emphasize choice and the ability to opt-out of the process entirely.

The Implications for How We Communicate

The challenge for communicators in a PTE is that the tools and approaches that worked before are increasingly proving ineffective. We are now far away from the time when companies, salespeople, and politicians could tell their story and be heard, be listened to, even believed. And in this new world it is important to understand the new rules of engagement. What follows are seven lessons we have learned about what has changed in a PTE. Rather than being guidelines for how to communicate—that comes later in the book—these challenge old truisms that died with the end of trust.

1. The truth will not set you free. Once a lifeboat in the turbulent seas of controversy, truth has taken on too much water. Just because something is true doesn't mean it's going to gain trust, sell products, or buy you forgiveness. Often we cling to facts because, well, how can you argue with something that's factual and true? If it's true and it's on your side, you must be right. Wrong. Most communicators believe they can "set the record straight" if only they can get people to understand their point of view—the "truth."

The first problem with the truth in the PTE is that everyone has their own version. What you call a fact, I call one part of the story. When you say something is indisputably true according to the experts, I say, "which experts?" When you give me a statistic to prove your point, I can find one on the Internet to disprove it. When Nobel Prize–winning economists still can't agree on the causes and solutions to the Great Depression seventy-five years after the fact, it is clear that the facts have limitations.

The second problem with facts is that they often cause more harm than good by trying to tell a story that the audience fundamentally doesn't want to hear. Witness BP patting itself on the back for capturing 20,000 barrels of oil a day in June 2010, while acknowledging that at least 60,000 barrels a day would continue to flow into the Gulf in following months. Or Toyota trying to defuse a major safety crisis by citing the fact that 80 percent of all Toyotas sold in the past twenty years were still on the road. Or GM's advertising campaign touting repayment of their government loans "in full and with interest" while still holding billions of taxpayer funds from TARP. It doesn't matter if BP was making progress, if Toyota vehicles really do last forever, or if GM had paid back the American taxpayer.

The problem is that no one wants to hear it. The public calls them "half-truths." A half-truth does not pull a skeptic halfway toward your view. It pushes them farther away. It's a persuasion fatality. These are what I like to call "fatal facts."

Yes, they're true. Yes, they're logically sound. Yes, they make sense to you from your company's perspective. But their utility ends there. You can print out fact sheets and cite forces beyond your control all you want, but for the most part the public doesn't care. Facts that look like they're being used to rationalize or cover up bad behavior simply do not work. Instead, you must understand that in the PTE, people demand more. They want more explanation, more authenticity, more straight talk, and more accountability. Hiding behind the facts doesn't build trust any more than being not as bad as everyone else.

2. "Your Truth" is not what matters to people. Most organizations are an echo chamber for a point of view that is consistent with the organization's mission. It is more subtle than "drinking the Kool-Aid." Instead, it is an organization's worldview supported by facts, data, customer insights, and personal experiences. It is often combined with an internal lexicon made up of industry jargon, organizational acronyms, and other shorthand language that people outside the company can't easily grasp. Taken together, we call this "Your Truth."

Unfortunately, in almost every situation in which we have been involved, the organization's customers, critics, and the public have a different truth, supported by a different set of facts and experiences. We call this "Their Truth." The problem for many organizations is that they assume their view of the world is shared by others—that "Their Truth" is somehow *the* truth. In reality, they're wrong. What's important to understand is that only one view of the truth matters, namely the audience's.

Here's an example of how the financial services industry and the rest of the world looked at the financial crisis in early 2009.

Your Truth (Financial Industry Perspective)	Their Truth (Public's Perspective)
Not everyone in the banking industry was involved with toxic assets.	EVERYONE is to blame.
TARP funds are a small percentage of our capital.	It's ALL TARP funds.
Some institutions are actually doing okay.	You've failed AS AN INDUSTRY.

In other industries, the gaps are equally large. In politics we are used to this large gap in worldview from one end of the political spectrum to the other. This has not been true in the corporate world where companies believed that they understood their customers and knew how to market and communicate with them. But the reality is that working for a company changes the way you look at the world. And it makes it harder to effectively sell ideas or products because consumers look at the world so differently. From financial services to health care, from energy to food and beverages, the world looks completely different depending on where you sit. It is as though you are watching two different baseball games and trying to agree on the score.

Where communicators falter most, however, is in believing that once they understand the worldview of their audience they can somehow change it. You can't. If you want the public to agree with you, you cannot try to change their view of the truth. Instead, communicators must learn to accept the public's worldview and find messages and symbols that work within it. Take a typical major corporation: You can argue all day long that multimillion-dollar compensation packages are necessary to retain their best talent. But if that runs counter to someone's belief that senior executives shouldn't make more money while their shareholders and employees face huge cuts, you lose.

3. **The Fifth Amendment is a death sentence.** In a PTE, you are guilty until proven innocent. Silence is considered an admission of guilt. And every minute you fail to tell your own story is an eternity for critics to tell theirs. Tiger Woods is just one example of someone who thought erroneously that the story would go away if he just kept quiet about his womanizing ways. It used to be that a company would do something "bad," or a product would be recalled, or a CEO might get caught lying, but the information was relatively contained.

You had to buy the paper, turn on the news, or hear about it from a friend. Not so anymore. Now you're likely to see a link to the story in your Twitter feed, hear about it through your podcast, see it on the TV in the elevator at your office, or get a text alert on your phone. And it all happens instantly, without delay and before spin has had a chance to muddy the water. We have more access to more information than ever before, and as a result we see everything happen in real time—the good, the bad, and most certainly the ugly.

4. You can only tell one story. It used to be that marketing could tell one story to customers, human resources could tell another to employees, and investor relations could tell yet another to stockholders. These stories weren't different in substance necessarily but you can bet that many companies talked about their reasons for layoffs differently depending on the audience.

Today, that just doesn't fly. The Internet, twenty-four-hour news cycles, and the explosion in social media mean the silos have disappeared and that what you say to one audience will be heard by the other audiences as well. And critics love to find your own inconsistencies and turn them against you.

5. You are often your least credible source. I've told countless clients that no matter how truthful their information is, the fact that it comes from *their* website, *their* press release, or *their* spokesperson immediately gives it the stench of corporate spin and hidden agenda. People are especially suspicious of anyone engaged in horn tooting, no matter what it's about.

6. Show and tell, but mostly show. In the past, words were often enough. Companies or politicians would spin a story and it would get them through a difficult situation. Or they would talk about their commitment to change for as long as it took the media to move onto the next story. Today, words matter more than ever. But they're not enough on their own. My firm specializes in finding the right words to help companies effectively and credibly communicate just about anything, but we must often make it clear to our clients that words in the absence of deeds—meaningful deeds with symbolic value—will fail. It is one thing for the CEOs of firms like JP Morgan Chase, Bank of America, and US Bancorp to sit in front of Congress and admit they bear responsibility for the financial crisis. It is quite another for them to take the actions that demonstrate—in ways that appeal specifically to external audiences—that they actually believe it.

It doesn't take an expert to understand that saying the right thing only gets you so far. After all, telling your parents repeatedly you'll clean your room when you're a kid only works so many times: eventually you have to pick up your stuff and actually clean your room.

People want to see companies demonstrate responsibility. They want to see how those companies have changed their practices so the same mistakes don't happen again. They want evidence that you understand your broader responsibilities to customers and the public. If you cannot point to specific examples of how you are making your actions align with your rhetoric, you will be called on it.

This tangible evidence allows you to create your own symbols to combat all the negative ones. If done right, it lets you turn a weakness into a strength. For example, a financial services firm should create a new lending model for Americans that celebrates the loans it *doesn't* make. That firm would have the opportunity to separate itself from the pack as the "responsible bank." Likewise, when a food service company has a cleanliness scandal, it should not forget the incident: It should use it to show the public how the company is ensuring that this doesn't happen again. In fact, it should probably make its response a visible part of its business, to demonstrate its leadership in protecting its food supply.

By putting your money where your mouth is, you can create your own meaningful symbols to communicate your positive messages and/or combat those being used against you. And in the examples mentioned previously, fighting fire with fire is far more effective than walking into the blaze holding a well-polished speech.

7. **Institutions must stand for something.** Now more than ever, companies must actively think about what their brands symbolize to the public. Relying on stellar sales or impressive stock performance may have worked in the past, but today that will lead to consumer resentment. In the PTE, successful companies must be more than profitable—they must do good, give back, and take responsibility. If they don't, their financial success will come back to haunt them.

For some companies, a positive image is built into the brand. The name Johnson & Johnson, while a huge, vastly diversified company, more often than not makes you think about baby products. It makes you think about family, quality, and care. They have a history of providing the things families need, from the littlest to the biggest. Literally, the products they provide offer consumers peace of mind and confidence. Sure, they'll face their share of problems, but Johnson & Johnson's strong brand has a positive image that will, in many cases, give it the elusive immunity that can only be provided by that rare bird, "benefit of the doubt."

Ironically, Johnson & Johnson is alone among its peers in the pharmaceutical industry. For all the lives the industry saves, the pharmaceutical industry has done a poor job creating strong positive imagery around its companies or the industry as a whole. Their products routinely allow Americans to enjoy more birthdays and an increasingly higher quality of life. Yet they are constantly beaten up, attacked from all sides, and increasingly regulated by those in power. Why? Because they thought their products would speak for themselves. On the path to selling those products they ignored the concerns of key stakeholders and lost the trust of the public. Today, when you talk about the reputation of a pharmaceutical company, the public will definitely talk about profits, TV ads and four-hour erections, and drug side effects. What they are less likely to talk about is the way the pharmaceutical industry has changed the face of medicine. Because the industry has not defined its image around its positive impact on the world, pharmaceutical companies have been defined by their profits. And they now find it exceedingly difficult to tell any of the many positive stories they want to tell.

Instead of stemming from quality products and services, sometimes positive brand images come from the way companies operate their businesses. Starbucks has long been known for the way it treats its employees well, Whole Foods for how it does good things for the environment and its people, Southwest Airlines for the way it treats its customers while delivering its product (flying people from A to B), Microsoft for its commitment to philanthropy (through the Gates Foundation), and JetBlue for the way its former CEO and two directors are creating customer goodwill by donating their salaries to a fund to help employees facing emergency hardships.

These are big companies, but their positive images are not a function of money. In fact, these are all highly successful and profitable companies, yet they don't face the same challenges pharmaceutical companies face. They represent examples of what is consistently a powerful symbol in this age of mistrust—the idea that the company has priorities other than the simple pursuit of profit.

* * *

My firm was built on the belief that "It's not what you say, it's what they hear." That simple saying has never been more true. In the PTE, *how* you communicate is just as important as *what* you communicate. The old rules no longer apply. A new approach to communicating is needed—one specifically built around the need to address a skeptical public. If you don't use the language of trust that recognizes your target audience's concerns and the baggage they bring to the table, you will rarely succeed in getting the outcome you want or supporters you need.

2

It All Starts with Words

What if you are selling a good product, but the customers who would benefit most won't listen to your message?

What if you are doing the right things, but your audience still won't give you credit?

What if you end up on the wrong side of a news story and you need to set the record straight?

Countless frustrated clients have come to us with these questions. They have made great efforts to reduce their carbon footprint and ecological impact, yet continue to be viewed as bad environmental actors. They place a real and determined emphasis on product safety, yet become defined by a single negative news story based on a questionable scientific study. They have great products to sell, but are shackled by misconceptions. Skepticism is so strong and prevalent that many of my clients find new meaning in the phrase "no good deed goes unpunished."

The language of trust is designed to help you—as a salesperson, corporate executive, employer, or even an individual—find the right language to address situations where there seems to be a "failure to communicate." I've built my career and my company around learning how to uncover language to overcome skepticism and engage an audience that doesn't agree with me. What I have learned is that the right language is always there. You simply have to find it. Now that doesn't mean you can always sell ice to Eskimos, but it does mean you can at least get the Eskimos to take off their earmuffs and listen to your sales pitch. More often than not, the right message can be the currency that buys you a seat at the table. And in a PTE knowing what to say and how to say it is the first step to making sure your invitation doesn't get lost in the mail.

Make no mistake that communicating with trust is about much more than words. It involves the way we think, and the way we act. But it *starts* with words—and those who learn the language of trust are the ones who will hold the keys to success in the new era.

The combined effects of skepticism and accessibility—24/7 access to information en masse—contribute to a consumer audience that just won't listen . . . to you, at least. People have made up their minds about everything from their position on PC versus MAC and Pepsi versus Coke to their opinions on Wal-Mart. In each case, these opinions are rooted in a worldview that individuals have developed over their lifetimes. And most of the information that they seek and, more important, hear is information that gels with their existing beliefs. Everything else gets blocked out. Consider the detail with which markets are segmented today. There is a newspaper, a magazine, an RSS feed, a blog, a Twitter feed, a cable network, and a Facebook fan page that caters to *you* as a consumer. You hear the news you agree with, see advertisements for the products you want to buy, and see the TV shows that support your interests and hobbies. It took a while to get there, but news and information are now more customizable than cars or clothing. You don't have to listen to anything or anyone else if you don't want to. Don't like what you're hearing? Change the channel. Click "block sender." Check out.

This is another reason why a new language of trust is necessary. Not just because people are skeptical of sales language or are critical of corporate messages, but because they are able to avoid them altogether. More than ever before, people have the freedom and power to shut you out, and shut you up. The only way to talk to your audience—or in many cases, just to steer a conversation in your direction—is to adopt a new kind of language. Your language must be strategic, authentic, humble, and receptive to opposition. You must find the communication "truth-space" where what *they* believe aligns with what *you* are saying. It is in this common ground that you can begin to connect with skeptics.

The language of trust is the language of your audience. Over and over again, clients come to us with messages that represent exactly what they want to say, with little consideration given to whether it is a message that the audience wants to hear. The language of trust isn't about *you*, the communicator. It is about the audience—their needs, their concerns, their fears, their hesitation, their need for truth and information.

An advertisement decades ago showed a serious-looking independent insurance agent staring into the camera and saying, "I might not sell you Crum & Forster insurance even if you ask for it." No, he wasn't crazy. He was just ahead of his time. This independent agent was committing to always taking the side of the customer, not of the insurance companies he represented.

And in 2006 Tylenol launched a campaign that many people would call crazy—telling people not to take the product if they didn't use it responsibly. One TV spot featured Brenda Bass, vice president of sales for Tylenol, speaking into the camera: "Some people think if you have a really bad headache, you should take extra medicine. Problem is, that's not going to get rid of your headache faster. And taking too much of any medication, no matter how safe it is, can cause serious problems. Your health is important to us, so if you're not going to take the recommended dose of our medicine, I'd rather you just didn't take it. And if that means selling less Tylenol, that's fine with me."[4] In reality, this didn't hurt sales and it did reinforce the reputation of the makers of Tylenol as a responsible company that could be trusted with your family's health.

To overcome skepticism, all communicators need to become agents for the customer, even though their paycheck has the name of a specific business on it. In fact, especially when it does. We now live in an era that gives new meaning to the Biblical injunction that "he who exalts himself shall be humbled, and he who humbles himself shall be exalted."

Consider the success of Southwest Airlines. Even in a time when commercial airlines are in the red, folding after decades in business, Southwest has remained a bastion of profit and success—much to the chagrin of their competition. What have they consistently provided since their inception? Not customer service—anyone can provide that—but rather, customer advocacy. They don't simply want passengers to get from point A to point B—they want them to get there for the lowest cost, in the shortest amount of time, with the least hassle. What's more, they want those customers to feel good about their experience. (Is it any coincidence that their stock symbol is LUV and their drink stirrers are heart-shaped?) Their employees are empowered to advocate for their customers, and their shareholders reap the rewards.

The language of trust puts control in the hands of your audience. Though the goal of every one of our clients is to sell something—an idea, a product, a brand—the path of least resistance is often not to sell at all. As counterintuitive as this may seem, we have found that the nature of the decision-making process has changed. The fastest way to get someone to buy your product is to give them objective information and let them make up their own mind. The classic salesperson "close" doesn't work anymore. Instead, it raises the level of skepticism and makes the real close that much harder. Remember, the premise of this book is that you have something that you are trying to sell that is worth buying. When that is the case, your language needs to let your product or idea and the competition compete on a level playing field—a field where your product or idea should come out the victor.

"Give me a salesperson I can trust, not a salesperson who says, 'Trust me.'" I don't know who said it, but this statement perfectly illustrates the problem of trying to sell too hard in the current environment. "Trust me" is about the worst thing that you can say if you want to gain trust. But there is a whole lexicon of other words and phrases that do equal damage.

For example, in our work in the financial services industry, we have found that the most effective financial advisors rarely need to talk about products. In initial conversations with a client, they may never utter the word "equity," "annuity," or "fund." Instead, they focus on building credibility and a trusting relationship. In doing so, the burden of making final recommendations and decisions about the specific products becomes secondary. Selling is about building trust, then offering the facts in a neutral, nonintimidating way and allowing the consumer to decide.

Now let's take it a step further. We not only have our radar up for the integrity of the products and services we use, but also the *words and phrases* used to describe them. In our work on variable annuities we found that every time we talked about "guarantees" or tried to push investors to act with phrases like the "risk of not acting," the reactions were strongly negative. Why? Because these words are triggers: One sounds like the overpromising rhetoric of traditional sales, the other tries to scare the listener. Both fall flat.

But when the same person starts using phrases like "an option for protecting a portion of your assets," our research shows that consumers start listening. A word like "option" leaves control in the hands of the customer. And using the word "portion" immediately reduces the risk associated with a decision to invest money in a new financial product. By using these words, the financial advisor is viewed more as an ally who will help them find the best, most secure investment option. There is no "close," just honest, straightforward communication. Ask baristas at Starbucks, Tully's, Seattle's Best, and Caribou Coffee where to find the best latte in town. Guess what they will answer. In all likelihood you'll find yourself feeling pretty silly for having asked in the first place—of course they will pick their own brand or shop. Did you learn anything? Did you get any information you didn't already have? Unlikely. This is the story of nearly everyone who sells a product, a service, or an idea. Unfortunately, as we've learned, this approach is outdated—a dinosaur left from a less skeptical time.

Now let's imagine one of these baristas has read this book, and what's more, her manager and trainer are also well versed in the new language of trust (insert shameless book plug here). She would give you a very different response. She would tell you in detail about her store's lattes—what they do well, and where they miss—and also about their competitors. She might tell you that Starbucks makes a seasonal gingerbread latte, while Caribou Coffee has a great frozen option. She might even suggest a local independent shop. In the process of giving you this information—a fair, fact-based approach—she gains your ear and your trust. And in all likelihood, your business.

Shifting gears from the coffee wars to your own business, does this mean you should start recommending your competitors to people? Some businesses like retail clothing giant Nordstrom do exactly that. When they don't have what a customer wants—the right fit, the right brand, the right color—they often help customers find what they need elsewhere. The goal is satisfaction and a trusted relationship, not sales. Again, this counterintuitive "sales" technique has led it to a path of consistent growth through economic ups and downs.

If talking up direct competitors seems a little wild to you—or if it really isn't an option in your field—you can still put your customer in control by offering customers neutral information. Give them the facts about your product. Tell them the limits of your technology or your service. Let them know what you do better than anyone else. And then, step back and let them decide.

The language of trust is authentic. The only way to appear honest and authentic in the PTE is to *be* honest and authentic. If you try to adopt the principles of communication outlined in this book but your actions cannot live up to the expectations you set with your words, then your personal or corporate credibility will erode at a staggering pace.

That type of mismatch adds fuel to the skeptic's fire—a fire they are happy to fan in your direction. As I've said before, show and tell—but mostly show. Give people reasons to trust you—your outstanding products, your impeccable service delivery, your "customer-first" attitude—and they will be more likely to listen to your message.

Take the example of Monro Muffler Brake, a Rochester, New York–based chain that has become the most profitable independently owned under-car repair operation. Many chains have slogans that tout their honesty, as does Monro (in their case, "Only what you need, done right the first time, guaranteed"). But in addition, it has a list of specific action items that employees follow posted in each of its stores, under the name of "The Monro Doctrine." Some of these action items include:

- A service technician and a supervisor will independently inspect your car and agree on an estimate.

- They will call for approval first before repairing any issues that they discover after starting work.

- They will match lower prices on the same work for a thirty-day period.

Monro does not provide words in lieu of deeds; it provides words to describe deeds. There is no spin, no ad-speak. There is just credible information to back up actions.

The post–World War II era ushered in a period of mass advertising where slogans and claims—the louder, the better—drove our purchasing behavior. Now in the PTE, you have to "show them the money" before customers will show you their money. This means that while your words are more important than ever, actions speak louder than words. Like Monro, you need to express these actions when you communicate so your words have something to stand on.

The language of trust recognizes that we all have flaws. The obvious drawback to authenticity is, of course, your flaws. You can't hide them anymore. The skeptical consumers of the PTE are already asking friends, scouring the Internet, and doing everything they can to uncover those flaws before they develop a case of buyer's remorse.

They have more and more resources at their disposal to get second opinions, double-check facts, and find independent reviews. Put simply, bad facts about your products and companies are out there, and denying them is no longer an option. Luckily for you, the language of trust is built around the idea that you can have an imperfect product or company and still attract and retain customers. In fact, in many cases fallibility actually builds credibility.

To err is human. To acknowledge your shortcomings is divine. Consumers don't expect any product or company to be perfect. The very notion is laughable. They're not perfect and they have never purchased a product that is perfect, so they don't expect you to be either. Rather than flocking to products that overhype their benefits, skeptical consumers are turned off by superlatives. By denying your fallibility you become "the other." You become something that cannot possibly exist, which makes it that much easier for consumers to dismiss and discredit you. The result is the very opposite of what you would hope to achieve.

Instead, if you acknowledge last year's product recall, the front page exposé in the *New York Times*, or the one-star reviews on Amazon .com, you can start to talk about how you're going to fix those problems moving forward. You can talk about how you've learned from your mistakes and how you want to make things better. You will regain trust, build credibility, and become more believable because you've accepted your imperfections and decided to move forward. If this seems like a stretch, consider the classic job interview question, "Describe your strengths and weaknesses." A prospective employer is not looking for an angelic response—"I'm almost *too* organized"—but instead wants real insight into your professional flaws. They want to see that you have acknowledged and accepted those weaknesses, *and that you are working to improve.*

If You Can't Beat 'Em, Join 'Em

Have you ever been to a grocery store where customers are free to post notes saying, "Don't buy this brand of soup" or "This cereal is the best"? You have if you have ever purchased groceries online at Amazon.com. It built its massive online storefront around the idea that you are part of a community of purchasers who talks to each other.

The online product rating revolution means that whatever your marketing department says about your product or service, yours is just one opinion among many. Today, few people purchase big-ticket items like computers, cars, or vacations without first checking out their ratings on the Internet. And this movement has quickly gone down-market to everything we buy: recently on the ratings website Epinions.com, for example, nearly thirty people posted ratings and commentary for one children's book published in 1978, while Amazon.com has over one thousand reviews of a household iron.

This trend means that if you are still stuck in the mind-set of generating hype about your products, you risk getting flattened by the opinions of real consumers. But, if you start to see yourself as an unbiased information provider, you have a chance to become part of the dialogue.

The language of trust validates objections. In the past, sales were about "overcoming objections." Your customer talked, you "listened," and you responded with a list of reasons to dismiss their concerns. You may have even said something like, "What you need is safety and security in an automobile," or "What you want is great taste with fewer calories." In the PTE, this technique falls flat. Today, if a salesperson responds to a concern by—gasp—telling the customer what they want, they might be dismissed outright.

The healthy skepticism you face today requires *validation*, a process that is the polar opposite of "overcoming objections." It means using words to let people know that their concerns are *valid*. Acknowledging what you hear, and asking people what they want. Validation is the key to a fresh, new way of creating dialogue with the people you connect with and sell to.

Imagine you're a life insurance broker, and a prospect, let's call her Jane Smith, says, "I'm still young. I can't stand the idea of spending so much money on life insurance," in response to your efforts to sell her some. Old-school sales techniques prescribe overcoming this objection with reasons about why life insurance is a good thing. Rather than really listening to what the prospect is saying, and what she's concerned about, you're supposed to marshal all the arguments in favor of life insurance and be ready to counter her objections. You say things like, "What you need is . . ." and "What you want is . . ." In the PTE, this approach makes you look like a Wall Street vulture rather than an advocate.

A better approach would be to listen carefully and acknowledge Jane's concerns. Tell her you felt the same way when you had to make personal finance decisions, and once you learned more about life insurance you realized it wasn't always right for everyone. You tell her that in her case, buying even a small life insurance policy would provide peace of mind for her family in the unlikely event something happened to her.

Suddenly you're not on offense, Jane's not on defense. The two of you are simply having a conversation about the right approach for her unique situation. You've put her in control by validating her concerns and offering facts and information so she can make the right decision.

Let's use a politically charged example—health care reform. You believe that it is a crime for a country like the United States not to offer affordable, quality health care to all Americans. Your neighbor opposes health care reform with equal conviction because she believes that individuals do not have a right to health care but they should have a right to decide whether or not to purchase health insurance. Imagine the conversation that ensues. You try to overcome her objections. You find ways to convince her how wrong she is by throwing out facts and figures and holding up other countries as examples. You spend more time talking than listening. She digs her heels in, and you both walk away angry.

Now consider validation. Instead of trying to convince her that she is intrinsically wrong and that you are morally right, you acknowledge the things you have in common—the facts that you both agree on. You find that you both believe health care costs are far too high in America today and that much of health care spending is being spent in the wrong places. In the process, you start a meaningful dialogue—one where you can both agree with reducing the need for something no one likes.

In both of these cases, you are using new words—namely *their* words—to create a relationship of trust. Your part of the dialogue no longer contains words such as "wrong," "better," or "opposing." Now it reflects the other person's concerns with terms like "reasonable," "understandable," and "important." It starts with what you agree on. In the process, you change from being a partisan with an agenda to someone who lives where your listeners live, and experiences what they experience. You build a relationship based on trust.

The New Sales Mantra: Agree with Objections

Scott West purchased a piece of expensive name-brand luggage, a brand he trusted for years. But this time, he found that some of its components that were formerly steel had been replaced with rubber.

When Scott complained about this to the salesperson, he replied, "I have been selling this line of luggage for twelve years, and when I noticed this, I shared my concerns with the company as well. Here is what they told me: They are trying to balance cost against factors such as weight, given how flying has changed. I respect whatever is important to your decision about what to buy." This authentic, information-oriented response to skepticism generated instant trust and credibility—as well as a purchase.

This salesperson was speaking from the heart. He was also giving accurate, factual information to inform the customer's purchasing decision. But he also did something that many traditional salespeople never, ever do: he used an objection to build trust, by using it to see the situation through the eyes of the customer, and advocate for the customer's interests.

Engaging the Skeptic

The mind-sets of people who receive your messages fall within a continuum, with optimists at one end, pessimists at the other end, and skeptics in the middle:

- Optimists are easy to identify and communicate with. They are a shrinking group.

- Pessimists are, in a sense, easy to communicate with as well. They have a toxic level of negativity, and should be generally avoided rather than engaged. In most situations, if they are against you, nothing you can say will change their mind.

- Skeptics, who make up the majority of us, are people who fit the dictionary definition described earlier. They represent a healthy challenge to status quo, and tend to delay judgment until they gather more facts and information. They are your target.

Healthy skepticism is something that can be understood and managed. Your overarching goal is to create meaningful dialogue with a skeptic, based on the following four principles of credible communication:

Be Personal
Be Plainspoken
Be Positive
Be Plausible

Each of these principles underscores the fundamental contrarian nature of addressing skepticism that forms the core of this book: agreeing with skeptics and providing information to them rather than "overcoming their objections." What follows is a brief introduction to each of the four principles—principles that we will fully explore in later chapters.

Be Personal

There are many reasons why Barack Obama won the Democratic primary and Hillary Clinton didn't, but one of the most important was the simple fact that Obama ran a campaign about what "we" could do, and Hillary ran a campaign about what "she" could do. In a simple content analysis that I completed during the course of the primary campaign, I found that candidate Obama used the word "we" about six times more often than he used the word "I." At the same time, Clinton's ratio was nearly the opposite. Obama's campaign was about "yes, we can." Clinton's was about "strength and experience to make change happen" (among other slogans along the way). While Obama brought people into his campaign and gave them a role to play bigger than their vote, candidate Clinton ran a campaign that was much more about her than about our collective future.

For all of us, selling ideas or products or ourselves begins with a need to talk about something that we have and that the audience should need, want, or agree with. The problem is that too often, we focus on the first part—what we want to sell, and too little on the second—why they want to buy. Our language becomes internally focused. It is developed inside the four walls of a corporate organization. It uses acronyms completely unfamiliar to anyone who doesn't work at the organization. It sounds great to other people inside the organization. But it is largely irrelevant to the target audience.

And yet, our audience demands increasingly that messages, products, and services speak directly to them. The PTE consumer drives in a vehicle she customized at the dealership, is never afraid to ask for changes to a menu item at her local restaurants, and created a custom pair of sneakers for her child's last birthday present. She orders custom coffee from Starbucks or Dunkin' Donuts or McDonald's (Venti, quad cap, extra bone dry), owns a pink iPod (initials engraved on the back) with all of her—and only her—favorite music on it, and argues with the cable company about why she has to pay for some of the channels that she never watches. The things she consumes—buys, wears, drinks, eats—are all personalized in some form or another. She barely remembers a time when phones only had a single ringtone or when credit cards didn't carry images of loved ones on the front. This hyperpersonalization has led to its expectation. Consequently, not only do customers want more from products, services, and the companies that provide them, they also demand more from you as communicators. Namely, they demand personalized messages.

Consider the emails that arrive in your inbox, week after week—form letters practically screaming "insert name here." Do you spend more than five seconds considering whether to delete them? Probably not. If you're like most people we have surveyed, you hit "Report Spam" before giving it a second thought. These marketing ploys lack customization, and therefore lack personalization.

Now consider an example of individual branding. Imagine you are interviewing a potential employee. The applicant—Joe—is applying to be a plumber on your construction team. He is dressed appropriately, makes eye contact, and shakes your hand firmly. But when you start asking him questions about his qualifications and his career goals, he begins to lose your interest. He says things like, "I'm a team player" and "I want to improve my skills in bathroom sink installation." He's not saying anything *wrong*, he just isn't saying anything about *you*. If Joe had taken a cue from this book, he would have been prepared to turn those answers toward you—his audience. He would have said he could contribute to *your* team by bringing his expertise. He would have focused on you and how your company would benefit from having him on board. In short, he would have personalized his message to include his audience—*you*. And a simple change like that could make the difference between a job offer and a wave out the door.

Personalization is critical because it answers the question of "what's in it for me?" It helps the consumer understand why the issue matters to them or how the product will help them. It is incredibly obvious and yet consistently overlooked. But it is one of the most powerful tools we have in our arsenal to build trust.

Be Plainspoken

John McCain	Newt Gingrich
"Over thirty states have some form of 'high-risk' pool, and over twenty states have plans that limit premiums charged to people suffering an illness and who have been denied insurance."	"Transforming health and health care is urgent, because it is about saving lives and saving money. […] The urgency comes from the ability to save thousands of lives every year if only we would transform the system to take advantage of the technology available to us right now."

If you heard Senator John McCain and former Congressman Newt Gingrich talking about health care, who would you trust more? Which of these two is speaking in a language that is more compelling? Which one makes you more excited about the issue—more passionate about its outcome? And which one connects with you more on an emotional level?

If you're like most of the participants in our focus groups, you chose Newt Gingrich. His simple, straightforward call to action is far-reaching and universal. His message is clear; his words are to the point. No matter which side of the aisle you're on, you can agree that "saving lives and saving money" is important—even if you may disagree with him on how to achieve that goal. At least he grabbed your attention and has you listening.

And why do we think John McCain lost in 2008? Clearly not because of this statement alone, but his opponent's messages sounded more like Gingrich's. McCain's message, while similar in content and equally as valid, is lost in the minutiae of " 'high-risk' pools" and wonky jargon. Rather than appealing to people on a personal level, he relies on facts and logic without contextualizing the problem in a human way. Rather than speaking the language of Joe the Plumber, he speaks the language of Joe the Lobbyist. Not a recipe for success.

Not long ago, in a land not so far away, people equated sophisticated language with credibility. Today, however, that same jargon-filled, factoid-laden speech comes across as out of touch. More often than not, when you try dazzling someone with how smart you are, they don't buy it. Either they feel like you're trying to intimidate them, or they think you're trying to pull the wool over their eyes. Regardless, it's an approach that used to be both popular and successful, but now it simply no longer works.

In the PTE, communicators must sound like experts without talking like them. William Butler Yeats once said, "Think like a wise man, but communicate in the language of the people." If Yeats were around today—besides having an enviable number of Twitter followers—he would undoubtedly be well suited to communicate in the PTE.

Creating trust requires creating clarity. In the absence of clarity, confusion and frustration take root. When this happens, often what you say is lost to what they hear.

Make It Easy to Understand . . . or Else

Gary DeMoss, an avid boater, learned the importance of plain English the hard and expensive way. When Gary was still new to boating, he was having difficulty docking his new boat due to an unusually strong 6-knot current at the marina. His neighbor and longtime boater jumped on board and offered to help.

With Gary at the helm and his wife and children on board, Gary's neighbor talked him through the process—using nautical jargon. "Port, starboard, stern, thrusters!" Gary tried to translate as he maneuvered the boat, but the jargon came too fast and frequent. Gary misinterpreted his neighbor's jargon and hit forward throttle—running over a piling and slamming into his neighbor's boat. It was a $15,000 lesson on the importance of using plain language.

In this case, a lack of clarity led to a boat crash. Metaphorically speaking, the same thing happens every time you try to talk to a customer or prospect in language they don't understand. And because they probably don't pay as much attention to your industry or issue as you do, there is much more that they don't understand than you might think. That's why it is critical to test your language with someone from outside your company or organization. Only then can you see where the gaps in understanding really are.

Be Positive

Imagine you are eight years old again, cautiously eying your plate of spinach and peas at the dinner table. You fervently hope that the spinach and peas will miraculously disappear. They don't. You begin to panic, and try to catch the dog's eye. Just as you are about to escape this horrible fate, your mother turns to you and says, "Eat your vegetables, or you won't get any dessert."

Even at eight years old, we were all budding skeptics. We didn't appreciate fear tactics and strong-arm sales pitches. We wanted compassion, sympathy, and information. Why do I have to eat the spinach and peas? If they're good for me, why do they taste so bad? Why can't I have ice cream instead? We have questions, and we want answers— not raised voices and threats. We wanted mom to sympathize with us—tell us she hates peas, too. We wanted her to explain the positive health aspects of vegetables, the benefit of ice cream in moderation, and offer us a balanced solution: eat half the vegetables, get half the ice cream (or just forget the vegetables altogether).

Perhaps that much detail would have overwhelmed our eight-year-old selves, but today we crave it. What's more, we demand it. In the PTE—and really, in the years leading up until now—fear tactics have been eclipsed by much more successful, positive messaging.

Let's compare two basic messages for investing in variable annuities—an investment vehicle combining guaranteed income with principal growth—in the midst of uncertain financial times. First we will look at a typical fear-based sales message:

> I've been in the industry as a financial advisor for thirteen, almost fourteen, years now. So I have seen firsthand how annuities can benefit my clients. When 2000 rolled around, I knew a lot of people were retiring at that point, including my own mother. She had done extremely well. She had accumulated a lot of assets. And then in 2000, she lost 20 percent of her assets in one year. Three years later, half her portfolio was gone. And today, she is still working to make up for the losses she endured back then. When I sit down with my clients, this is a personal example I use to show the importance of annuities. Annuities are more than a pure investment. They are an investment with an insurance element that protects your assets. That way, if the market goes down in your later years, you aren't going to have to continue working through your retirement years to try and make up for what was lost.

This argument sounds logical. But over and over, our research shows it doesn't work. It "disturbs" in the traditional sense, but it also turns people off the speaker. People do not want to buy from someone who tries to use fear or scare tactics to sell them a product. They are reminded of that plate of spinach and peas.

Now before I am accused of trying to discredit one of the world's oldest sales techniques, let me give a bit more context. It would be wrong to say that fear tactics never work. In fact, they work especially well when you are trying to rally a group that already supports you, as in political fund-raising or get-out-the-vote efforts. But when you are trying to change skeptical minds, their track record is less impressive. For example, behavioral finance research has shown that fear of making the wrong choice is a key driver of inertia for investors. Rather than being motivated to act—to invest— fear tactics create paralysis. People would rather do nothing than do something wrong. I see this same reaction in many other situations as well. Try to scare someone into buying a product and they are likely to reject you and your tactics rather than buy into the fear.

Trust is built around the words you use, and words that invoke fear are triggers that destroy trust. If you want to communicate with skeptics, you need a different approach. One that focuses less on what the salesperson wants to sell and more on what the customer or client wants to hear:

It's natural to become more averse to risk as we get older. With unpredictable markets and retirement approaching, many investors shift their assets into more conservative investments like CDs and bonds. But this cautious approach often means that you completely miss the opportunity to grow your real assets in retirement. Annuities help you manage the risk of inflation while also giving you the opportunity to earn more than inflation. Annuities help you manage the risk of inflation by ensuring that your initial investment will grow at a guaranteed minimum percentage every year. Regardless of the market, your money grows by that percentage.

This message combines many of the elements of the new language of trust. It shifts the playing field from fear to benefits. And if you read it carefully, it also does something that few sales approaches do: It acknowledges why people often *don't* buy this product. Then it presents neutral, factual information to help the reader make up his or her mind. No threats of lost retirement, no subjective comparisons to competitive products, and no spin or superlatives. Just data. And, more important, just *positive* data.

Be Plausible

> The Architect: *The first matrix I designed was quite naturally perfect. It was a work of art, flawless, sublime. A triumph equaled only by its monumental failure. The inevitability of its doom is as apparent to me now as a consequence of the imperfection inherent in every human being, thus I redesigned it based on your history to more accurately reflect the varying grotesqueries of your nature.*
>
> —*The Matrix Reloaded* (2003)

For those of you reading this who somehow missed the Matrix Trilogy, here's the quick recap: Machines have taken over the world, captive humans are their source of energy, and they keep people alive and "content" by creating a false reality in their minds. Here, Neo is learning about the world he has managed to escape—the Matrix—from its creator. In short, the first world the Architect created was too perfect. It was a utopia that humans wouldn't accept as reality because human history is a balance of life and death, growth and destruction, trust and betrayal, joy and pain, success and failure—a balance that makes it impossible for us to buy anyone's promises of a perfect . . . anything.

Because of this basic, intrinsic human need for things to square with reality, effective communication must occupy the space between pragmatism and perfection. It must push people to the edge without pushing them off. It must be good enough to sell it, but not so good they don't buy it. Ultimately, the answer lies in a word: plausibility.

In a PTE, plausibility becomes even more important. Our increased skepticism means that we reflexively reject promises that are too good to be true because we know they aren't. In the process of thousands of research sessions on topics as distinct as energy policy and consumer packaged goods we have found that, put simply, credibility is built on plausibility. And plausible language generally follows each of these four rules:

Don't oversell. Think you are the "best of breed" or the "greenest" or the "highest quality"? Better to tone down the language and exceed expectations than find that your superlatives are met with skepticism.

Don't be extreme. Republicans and Democrats like to live in a black-and-white world—and the cable news shows are able to effectively sell products to their core audiences based on their own brands of extremism. But in most cases where people are selling ideas or products, the target audience sees that topic in shades of gray. Overstating the problem is a tool used all the time to make a point. Yet more often than not extreme arguments fail to do anything other than preach to the converted and alienate everyone else.

Find room for other answers. Whether you are selling a financial services product or energy policy or many things in between, often the best way to become plausible is to communicate that you are not the only answer to a given problem. Variable annuities are more attractive when they are explicitly intended for only a "portion" of the portfolio. And biofuels become more acceptable when they are only "part of the solution."

Acknowledge the flaws that everyone believes exist. Take nuclear plant safety. If I want to be plausible, the last thing I want to do is argue that nuclear plants are 100 percent safe. Though it may be the truth, no one will believe it, and, as soon as I say it, I lose much of my audience. Instead, I can build trust and credibility by acknowledging up front that "nothing is 100 percent safe, but that nuclear plants take extensive steps to prevent the expected and prepare for the unexpected."

The Principles in Practice

Changing your language is hard. Many of the companies and communicators that we advise are so involved in their topic, it's impossible for them to see things from the public's point of view. The language of trust might run counter to your instinct. It also runs counter to the way many corporations and industry groups have traditionally dealt with controversial issues surrounding things like product safety and regulation. But this language goes far beyond that short slice of modern history where we could impress each other with superlatives or expertise, and into a new generation where honesty and authenticity are king.

Consider the massive Toyota vehicle recalls in late 2009 and early 2010. Sticking accelerator pedals and defective floor mats allegedly led to several high-profile accidents, some of which resulted in deaths. On February 9, 2010, Toyota President Akio Toyoda published a letter in the *Washington Post* apologizing for the malfunctions and outlining his company's response to the crisis. In it, he expressed his deep disappointment for the quality and safety issues, and brought out a number of facts to defend the company: the large number of Toyotas still on the road, the rarity of safety issues with their vehicles over the years, and the company's commitment to continuous improvement.

While this was a perfectly decent apology, the beginning and ending (the parts that should be the strongest) relied on "fatal facts"—facts completely inconsistent with the worldview of the audience. The *Washington Post* was flooded with angry responses, and Toyoda's testimony before Congress later that month was met with equal frustration and consternation.

Compare this to what JetBlue did a few years ago, when a February ice storm stranded thousands of airline passengers on JetBlue planes on airport tarmacs for up to nine hours, causing national outrage. Even after several days, the airline still had numerous operational problems that further infuriated its passenger base—and the American public.

Instead of sending out a boilerplate apology and refunding a few irate passengers, JetBlue's CEO at the time, David Neeleman, responded by introducing something no other airline had and that the public was clamoring for: a Passengers' Bill of Rights. This Bill of Rights was announced in a full-page ad that ran in twenty newspapers in fifteen cities. It included a letter signed by the CEO acknowledging that JetBlue was both "embarrassed" and "deeply sorry" for its role in the debacle.

JetBlue could have tried to hide behind something it couldn't control—weather—but it didn't. Instead, JetBlue acknowledged its failure and recommitted to putting people first.

These two leaders took radically different approaches to handle a PR crisis, and one clearly succeeded where the other failed. The best way to see this is to compare what they each said. Their *words* were what mattered. First let's look at an excerpt from Toyoda's *Washington Post* apology:

More than 70 years ago, Toyota entered the auto business based on a simple, but powerful, principle: that Toyota would build the

highest-quality, safest and most reliable automobiles in the world.
The company has always put the needs of our customers first and
made the constant improvement of our vehicles a top priority. That
is why 80 percent of all Toyotas sold in the United States over the
past 20 years are still on the road today.

When consumers purchase a Toyota, they are not simply purchasing a car, truck or van. They are placing their trust in our company. The past few weeks, however, have made clear that Toyota
has not lived up to the high standards we set for ourselves. More
important, we have not lived up to the high standards you have
come to expect from us. I am deeply disappointed by that and
apologize. As the president of Toyota, I take personal responsibility. That is why I am personally leading the effort to restore trust
in our word and in our products. . . .

But great companies learn from their mistakes, and we know
that we have to win back the trust of our customers by adher-
ing to the very values on which that trust was first built. The
hundreds of thousands of men and women at Toyota operations
worldwide—including the 172,000 team members and dealers in
North America—are among the best in the auto industry. Whatever problems have occurred within our company, the strength
and commitment to fix them resides within our company as well.[5]

Now let's look at the words of David Neeleman, CEO of JetBlue
at the time of the 2007 incident:

> Dear JetBlue Customers,
> We are sorry and embarrassed. But most of all, we are deeply
> sorry.

Last week was the worst operational week in JetBlue's seven-year history. Many of you were either stranded, delayed or had flights cancelled following the severe winter ice storm in the Northeast . . . Words cannot express how truly sorry we are for the anxiety, frustration and inconvenience that you, your family, friends and colleagues experienced. This is especially saddening because JetBlue was founded on the promise of bringing humanity back to air travel, and making the experience of flying happier and easier for everyone who chooses to fly with us. We know we failed to deliver on this promise last week.

We are committed to you, our valued customers, and are taking immediate corrective steps to regain your confidence in us. We have begun putting a comprehensive plan in place to provide better and more timely information to you, more tools and resources for our crewmembers and improved procedures for handling operational difficulties. Most importantly, we have published the JetBlue Airways Customer Bill of Rights—our official commitment to you of how we will handle operational interruptions going forward—including details of compensation. We invite you to learn more at jetblue.com/promise.

You deserved better—a lot better—from us last week and we let you down. Nothing is more important than regaining your trust and all of us here hope you will give us the opportunity to once again welcome you onboard and provide you the positive JetBlue Experience you have come to expect from us.[6]

Do you notice a difference emotionally? We notice a difference *linguistically*. Here are some of the things our research tells us about these words:

- Toyoda begins by talking about the product and the company, not the customer. JetBlue's Neeleman starts by admitting how "deeply sorry" his company is, tacitly acknowledging that they had let "you"—the customer—down.

- Toyoda's comments seek to minimize the significance of the crisis by placing it into a historical and process context. He, in effect, tries to deny everything that the public was feeling at the time—that this crisis demonstrated that Toyota had lost its way. Neeleman, on the other hand, does nothing to minimize customer frustration. If anything, he validates their anger, putting him on the same side as his customers.

- Toyoda begins and ends with the company: their quality standards and their commitment to return to greatness. Neeleman begins and ends with the customer: taking ownership for what went wrong and vowing to make it right.

If you take away only one thing from this book, let it be this: In this era of mistrust, words are more important than ever. It's not what you say, it's what they hear. What people heard from Toyota's president were words for Toyota and about Toyota. He chose the past over the present, the company over the customer, and "I" over "you." Neeleman spoke the language of trust. He advocated for the consumer, people listened, and JetBlue passed its own Passengers' Bill of Rights more than two and a half years before the federal government did so.

PART TWO

THE FOUR PRINCIPLES OF CREDIBLE COMMUNICATION

Most of us look at language as something that doesn't change much—sort of like how Cher and Dick Clark always look the same. We clearly don't discuss ideas of love or business quite the way Shakespeare did, but conversely we don't think of our words and sentence structure as growing, organic, dynamic parts of our larger culture. But they are. We often change the words we use to describe things. Just think about how outdated the words "stewardess" and "secretary" sound today. Try finding a "used-car" lot. They don't exist, having all been replaced by "certified preowned car dealerships." Words themselves change meaning as well. The word "artificial" used to mean "full of artistic skill." A "nice" person was someone who was ignorant. And a "demagogue" was defined as "a popular leader." There are millions of subtler but equally significant changes in the way we use and interpret language.

In our work, we have found that language often has a shelf life. Meanings come and go, even if the words themselves stick around indefinitely. But it is not just the words that change. The structure of our language and the nature of our conversations have also changed dramatically. Perhaps most important, the way we listen—or more accurately, don't listen—has been forever altered.

In the PTE, our language and the way we communicate must learn to keep up. As information consumers, we have built up a tolerance to the same approaches to communication that we have seen so many times before. We reject the bold-faced sales pitch. We laugh at the firebrand who proclaims that our future will be ruined if we don't buy what he is selling. And we tune out when salespeople or politicians judge us and tell us what we should think or do. All of these approaches have long histories of success in persuasion.

A world that once looked up to experts and complexity, believed in promises made, and responded to threats and fear now demands authenticity and simplicity. The messages and approaches that worked well in the past must be reevaluated in light of this new paradigm. The language of trust is built around just such a reevaluation.

The next four chapters go into greater depth on each of the four principles of credible communication: be personal, be plainspoken, be positive, and be plausible. These principles have emerged from an incredible range of research projects over the last decade. There are great differences between the messages that we use to talk about pharmaceuticals and energy or technology and beverages, but these principles apply regardless of industry or topic. They may not all apply in every project, but the consistency with which we see these ideas emerge from our work is one of the main drivers of our decision to write this book.

The principles are listed in an order that made sense from a presentation perspective, but they are not intended to be approached in a linear way. These principles are highly interrelated, and we often find that effective messages can be judged as such through the lens of more than one principle. In other words, if you develop effective personal messages, they will also be both plainspoken and positive. It is also not enough to get one of them right at the expense of the others. If you use very positive language but it is not plausible or plainspoken or personal, you will have no more success than if you used negative language to begin with. That is not to say that there are not exceptions to these rules—there will always be circumstances where you need to draw outside the lines. It does mean that you cannot simply choose one of the principles at which to excel and ignore the others.

3

Be Personal

The Personal Principle:
It's Not About You, It's About Them

The first rule of building trust is to accept the fact that selling a product or idea has little to do with your company, what you're offering, or your ideas. It has everything to do with your audience and what they believe, think, and want. If you don't begin the communication process from their perspective, you are going to have an extremely difficult time winning their trust.

For the last decade, some marketers have preached the idea of one-to-one marketing. The idea is for companies to make marketing feel like it is directed at the individual. It is based on the idea that customer segments have preferences and that offers can be targeted to those preferences in a more relevant way than mass appeals. But most marketers and salespeople never *really* personalize their message. Watch many advertisements on television. Too often we are reduced to a stereotype: the suburban housewife, the sports-crazed middle-age man, the older couple steering their rowboat into the sunset. Open a letter from the IRS, and it begins "Dear Taxpayer." And when you talk to most people who are selling something, you sense that they notice just two things about you: that you have a pulse and money to spend.

Personalizing your message is all about speaking to a person's individual situation rather than trying to put people in categories. It means focusing on micro concerns rather than macro issues. And it means using language that explicitly communicates an understanding of your audience's situation rather than a generic nod to a perceived need. In this sense, personalization goes far beyond a communication skill. It starts with *listening* first.

The idea of personalization is not new: You see it in everything from targeted financial seminars to the hotel desk clerk who uses your name. But it is a lesson too easily forgotten or too rarely remembered. Communicators—quite naturally—tend to default to what is comfortable—to *them*. They focus on what they want to say instead of thinking about how that relates to what their audience wants to hear. They focus on facts or features that talk only about the issue or product—while not addressing how it directly impacts who they're talking to. In short, they neglect to explain why their audience should care. And in the end, that's the only part that matters.

In our experience, there are four components of personalizing your message as part of building a relationship of trust:

- *Make it relevant.* Just because you think something is important doesn't mean your audience does. You may care about shoes or the latest software or the environment. That doesn't mean what you are selling is top of mind for your audience. Your first job is to make your message personally relevant to your audience.

- *Make it tangible.* Would you prefer to know that there are ten thousand active taxicabs in a city you visit or that the typical wait time for a cab is four minutes? Chances are the latter because it explains the fact in terms that relate to you.

- *Make it human.* Too many arguments are made using cold facts instead of personal stories. If you want your audience to connect with a product or an issue, you need to make it human by telling personal stories.

- *Make yourself real.* The fastest way to lose a skeptic is to make your message sound like fine print reads. If you want to build trust, you have to communicate as you would to someone you trust, with less corporate-speak and more authentic language.

Make It Relevant

I have had the good fortune of working with a great organization called Conservation International (CI) over the past few years. CI has been fighting for the environment for more than two decades, yet they still face the problem of overcoming a skeptical public around the world in their daily communication efforts. Part of their challenge, it became clear, was the organization's historical focus on "protecting biodiversity." Though a noble goal, we heard two things over and over again in our research: first, "what is biodiversity?" and second, "conservation is about critters and forests, not *me*." Skeptics could easily reject the call to participate in CI's efforts because they felt no personal connection to the cause. In every session, we found that the piece that was missing from CI's focus on the environment was people. Or, said another way, to make the environment relevant to more Americans, CI had to connect protecting the environment with people. And so we changed the language. Instead of only talking about the needs of ecosystems and urgency of protecting our biodiversity, we made the environment more relevant by connecting it more closely to us.

Today, if you go to CI's website, you will see a much closer connection between the environment and people. The tagline reads "People need nature to thrive." The mission states: "Every person on Earth deserves a healthy environment and the fundamental benefits that nature provides. But our planet is experiencing an unprecedented drawdown of these resources, and it is only by protecting nature and its gifts—a stable climate, fresh water, healthy oceans and reliable food—that we can ensure a better life for everyone, everywhere."[7]

I often see communicators fall into this trap. They see the world through their own lenses and fail to make their products or ideas, or even product features, personally relevant to their audience. Just because you as a communicator see value in something does not mean that your audience will. Your job is to think about what you are selling from their perspective and tell them why what you are saying matters.

The health care reform debates of 1994 and 2009 hold important lessons about the need for personal relevance in messaging. In both cases, the drive for "universal coverage" was the early rallying cry for reform. Statistics cited the huge numbers of uninsured in America and the fact that we were the only developed country in the world not to provide health coverage for all its citizens. But an interesting thing happened on the way to reform. You see, Americans *do* care about the uninsured.

But what mattered to people much more than universal coverage was the loss of their own coverage. Talking about the uninsured simply does not resonate as much as the visceral, palpable fear that those who have insurance today might soon be added *to* the 47 million who currently lack it. That is why, by late 2009, most of the health care debate had left that term "universal coverage" behind. Instead, the way to make the message of health reform relevant was to talk about the personal risks of the current health care system and how health reform would ensure that you would never be without coverage, even if you lost your job or had a health condition.

In a world of skeptics, the need for relevance is particularly great because of the ease of turning you off or tuning you out. As other marketers and other issues compete for the skeptics' attention, you have to do the work of connecting the dots for your audience. You need to tell the skeptics what is in it for them.

Make It Tangible

In the aftermath of Hurricane Katrina, I was asked to help the New Orleans tourism industry communicate to the public about coming back to New Orleans. It wasn't an easy task. The news media had done a great job of portraying the city as waist deep in water with debris floating down Bourbon Street even months after the flooding was gone. New Orleans had a great deal of work to do, but they had made a lot of progress and they deserved a fair hearing. As is often the case when selling an idea or a product, the industry had come up with a long list of facts designed to show that the city was up and running. What they had failed to do was to make those facts tangible enough for people to understand what it would mean to them. To engage the skeptics, we had to personalize the facts. Here are some hypothetical examples:

Statistic	Personalized Statistic
There are currently 10,000 active taxicabs in the city of New Orleans.	In New Orleans, the average wait for a taxicab is four minutes.
There are currently 25,000 hotel staff employed by the city of New Orleans.	There are currently two hotel employees for every guest.
Room service is back in 90 percent of the hotels.	Room service is available twenty-four hours a day in the hotels that you use.

When you hear the first set of statistics it is easy to say, "yes, but . . ." "Yes, but those taxicabs can't make it to where I am staying." Or, "Yes, but twenty-five thousand hotel staff is probably a tiny fraction of what there used to be; service will not be good." The personalized statistics removed those questions and gave the skeptic a reason to take the data more seriously.

The question for all of your fact sheets and feature pages and proof points should be how can I make this fact or feature or proof point personally meaningful for my audience?

Make It Human

One of the challenges in selling products and issues is that you are dealing with inanimate objects or intangible ideas. Product development teams may have used research and consumer insights to build products based on real consumer needs, but the end result is still a product or a service with a set of features. And issues still generally boil down to a desired policy action. Ironically, the closer you get to a final product or policy, the farther you often are from the initial research with consumers that helped define what people want. To make things worse, your company has been forced to operationalize the selling of that product or issue. And in doing so, they have created a set of internal processes and an internal nomenclature that reflects your internal culture. By the time you get to communications, the consumer or the voter has long been lost. As a result, communications often naturally reflect the process that you have been through. Anything that hasn't been branded for external use tends to retain internal language. And the people responsible for building the product or policy often want to ensure that the elements most important to them get communicated to the general public. Health care offers a great example.

One of my favorite criticisms of the health care industry is that it is an industry dedicated to personally helping people and yet its language is so impersonal. Here are just a few of the impersonal terms people in that industry use to distance themselves from their patients.

Instead of Calling Them . . .	They Call Them . . .
Doctors	Providers
Nurses	Practitioners
Hospitals	Delivery systems
Health conditions	Indications
Statements	EOBs
Health care companies	Payers
Your health insurance plan	PPOs, HSAs, or HMOs

The point is that the health care industry has done a great job of depersonalizing what it does, and it is a big reason why we love having access to health care but hate a lot of the people and companies responsible for giving us that care. There is really no need for this language and no excuse for the industry to continue to speak this way. Health care should be about a patient and a doctor. To connect with the public on health care issues, messages should be framed in terms of *"you, your family, and your health."* To rebuild trust, one of the most important things the industry needs to do is speak in the language of the patient in all that they do.

Rather than using impersonal language, building trust requires that you translate your language and communications into terms that are human, not clinical. Rather than talking about macroeconomic factors or national statistics, you need to tell human stories. It is better to tell a relevant, personal story about a single affected person than it is to say that millions of people are affected.

Personalizing Infrastructure

Infrastructure. The term itself is highly unemotional. Do you care about your "personal infrastructure"? Probably not. Do you care about your "home"? I suspect the answer is yes. Both terms refer to the same thing, but one is human and the other, well, not so much.

My firm has been asked to work with a variety of organizations over the past few years to engage the public on infrastructure projects and build support for new investments. What we have heard consistently is that the term "infrastructure" is neutral at best. In many cases it is even viewed negatively, as it is connected to wasteful government spending, bridges to nowhere, and stuff that never seems to work as it is supposed to. The problem is that our infrastructure is failing in many parts of our country. Even where bridges aren't failing down (as was the case in Minnesota in 2007), our country is littered with failing roads, schools, and water systems. And yet Americans tend to reject the idea of investing lots of money to fix these problems.

Part of the reason is that infrastructure has never been personalized. It has been a construction issue instead of a quality-of-life issue. We might lament the fact that roads and bridges are in disrepair, but we are motivated to act when we think about the personal impact that disrepair has on our day-to-day lives. So rather than talking about how old our bridges are, or threatening Armageddon if we fail to fix our water system, we told personal stories. We painted a picture of the day-to-day impact of poor infrastructure in terms of "lost patience," "lost time," and "lost opportunities." We asked the public to think about the personal benefits to them if they could spend less time in traffic and never worry about water pollution reaching their homes or beaches. The response was a much higher level of engagement on the issue and a higher levelof trust that change could make a positive difference in people's lives.

The other reason to make things human is that it helps to connect issues to people's current experiences. In work we have done on lawsuit abuse, we found that voters often didn't respond when we talked about skyrocketing malpractice costs and doctors finding that they could no longer afford to practice medicine. But we also learned that across the Midwest, large majorities of Americans personally knew a doctor that had left the state, was planning to leave the state, or was retiring early—all because of the increasing difficulty of practicing medicine given the fear and costs associated with malpractice litigation.

Words That Work

A popular breast cancer specialist here in Ohio, Dr. Rachel Johnson, retired from surgery this year because of high liability insurance premiums. Never the subject of a lawsuit, Dr. Johnson is sorely missed in a medical field where early diagnosis is everything. As one of Dr. Johnson's patients told the *Daily News*, "It is not melodramatic to say there will be women who will die because of this."

When we have to travel long distances to get the care we need, something is wrong with our system. When good doctors are leaving the area to practice in places that give them the ability to practice good medicine rather than defensive medicine, something is wrong with the system. The best way to ensure that we can get the care we need in a place that we can reach in a medical emergency is to reform the system and make sure that doctors like Dr. Johnson continue to help patients in our communities.

Your challenge is to turn facts into narratives and policies into stories. By doing so, you can help ensure that you engage your audience and give them reason to believe that you understand their needs.

Make Yourself Real

Think about the last time you watched a press conference where a politician or celebrity read a statement, or where your company's senior management read a new policy off a sheet of paper. Chances are it didn't do a great job of instilling trust. And yet company after company issues prepared statements in language that only a lawyer could love. As a lapsed lawyer, I fully respect the need to avoid creating legal liability with public communications. As a professional communicator, I reject the idea that this is the way it has to be. Companies can and must be human in the way they communicate. So can managers even when they are dealing with challenging situations. To build trust, every communication must demonstrate that it is coming from someone or some entity with the character to be trusted. Often doing so means going "off the script" or "going beyond the four corners of the issue," but that is exactly what you should do.

What does this mean in practice? It means that you need to put a "human" face on a corporate act. You need to make your company or yourself real, not some emotionless entity that speaks from a mindless script. Explain your motives. Outline your goals. Talk about the good things you do even when the point of your communication is something else. The goal is to give your audience a broader picture of what makes you or your organization human.

Perhaps the most important language change to make yourself real and build trust is to change the words "you" or "me" to "we" and "our." This simple change puts you on the same side of the table as your audience and changes the way your audience will perceive the whole conversation.

Building Trust Even When Reducing Staff

How much trust and goodwill can you build in a meeting to discuss cutting back your organization? A lot, apparently, when you choose the right words and follow your heart.

Beth Israel Deaconess Hospital in Boston, like many health care facilities, was facing a budget shortfall of nearly $20 million—a sum that normally translates to hundreds of layoffs. But after CEO Paul

Levy wandered the corridors of his hospital and watched his front-line employees helping patients feel good as they pushed their wheelchairs, served them food, and cleaned their wards—acts he equated to practicing medicine—he stood before a packed auditorium of employees and chose the following words to discuss the looming cuts:

> I want to run an idea by you that I think is important, and I'd like to get your reaction to it. I'd like to do what we can to protect the lower-wage earners—the transporters, the housekeepers, the food service people. A lot of these people work really hard, and I don't want to put an additional burden on them. Now, if we protect these workers, it means the rest of us will have to make a bigger sacrifice. It means that others will have to give up more of their salary or benefits.

The rest of his thought was drowned out by sustained applause from everyone in the audience. And within the next few days, emails started flooding into his office, from employees and entire departments, suggesting what they could cut back. Soon nearly $16 million of voluntary cuts were put into practice, based on these suggestions, so that more people could keep their jobs.

What was radical about this meeting was not the idea of shared sacrifice, but the idea of approaching employees in an atmosphere of trust and engagement. As one anonymous Beth Israel employee commented online, "It is not that it is such a brilliant idea to cut pay in order to reduce layoffs or any of the other ideas that were offered, but it is the fact that he has a policy of an open employee forum and an anonymous way to voice your opinion that is important . . . he has gauged the feeling of the employees and so this is what helps make their decisions the best they can be under the circumstances. We know that we will work to minimize layoffs while maintaining *excellent* patient care."

Indeed, this sense of trust carried over to Levy's internal communications as well—for example, his blog (runningahospital.blogspot .com) studiously avoided discussing the praise heaped on Levy in the press in the aftermath of this meeting, and focused on the specifics of how employees banded together to save the jobs of 450 people.[8]

Pulls at your heartstrings, doesn't it? Levy's appeal was so successful because it put his employees first. It was about them, not him. It was about people, not profit. It was about the front lines, not the corner office.

Personalizing your message does not require a complete overhaul of the way you communicate or operate your business. In fact, the most important elements are nuanced. They are seen in subtle changes in words and phrases. Look at some of the things hospital CEO Levy said in his short speech:

"I'd like to get your reaction"
"If we protect these workers"
"The rest of us"

He is engaging people first and speaking in terms of shared experience using terms like "we" and "us." These are principles we measure in our testing, and teach to our clients.

Changing "you" to "we" or changing the order of the words you communicate often doesn't involve changing the content at all. But the effects are often far-reaching—and in the case of this hospital represent the difference between breaking the spirit of your employees or harnessing their energy. The point is this: trust is earned or lost in simple ways that we communicate.

*   *   *

Too many companies think that the good things they do will speak for themselves. Starbucks has been doing incredible things for the environment and farmers for decades, yet it doesn't get credit for it because it didn't talk about it enough. Now, as I sit in a Starbucks writing this, I can look at my cup and read about Shared Planet. I get a more human picture of the company. Pharmaceutical companies have been investing in patient assistance programs for years to help low-income patients get access to the medications they need, but they never talked about it. Today, many pharmaceutical ads include something at the end advising people to call the company if they need help paying for their medicines. In both cases, the good deed preceded the PR. But communication of these efforts is essential to personalizing the company and giving it a heart—or more of a heart than people otherwise give it credit for.

4

Be Plainspoken

The Plainspoken Principle:
If They Can't Understand You,
It's Your Fault

Not so long ago, we lived in an era of expertise. The public and consumers were attracted to big words and complex concepts, whether or not they were supported by substance. If something was difficult to understand but confidently communicated, we assumed that it was our fault that we couldn't understand and often gave the communicator the benefit of the doubt. We trusted doctors who spoke in medical jargon. We listened to financial advisors who talked about financial concepts we didn't really understand. And we invested in companies whose business models we didn't really understand. This last point was particularly true during the dot-com boom of the late 1990s when companies would actively seek to create complex descriptions of their business because investors and customers were more likely to work with a "business-to-business marketplace for expert business intelligence" than an "online market research store."[9] In an era of expertise, sophistication was given the benefit of the doubt.

In a world of skeptics, the opposite is true. If I can't understand what you are telling me, it's your fault, not mine. If I am confused, I blame you, not myself. And if I have to work hard to understand your message, I am probably going to listen to someone else who makes it easier for me. In this environment, plain language and accessibility are critical to building trust.

Your English teacher was right all along, but not just for the reason you think. Most people think that plain language is a virtue of clarity. We can show you that it is really a virtue of *credibility*. You get one chance to be clear with people nowadays, and if you blow it, their trust in you goes out the window along with their comprehension. This is because they now put the burden of understanding squarely on your shoulders.

Writing and speaking plainly was a virtue we all grew up with. Our parents and our English teachers taught it to us. But then we grew up and started our careers. We became financial analysts discussing arbitrage, engineers speaking about MRP and CAD/CAM, or psychology professors referring to hermeneutics (which, ironically, is the interpretation of language). We started working at companies, became SVPs, worked with RSDs, created budgets during AOPs, planned strategies with KPIs, and then compared results with LY. We learned at least three new dialects: the industry dialect, the company dialect, and the job function dialect. And much like regional dialects in other languages, much of the communication is easy to understand, but key words and phrases are completely foreign to a listener from a different region.

Don't Be a Wonk

A large group of about four hundred financial advisors watch expectantly from the audience as twenty-five high–net worth investors sit on a stage with handheld dials in their hands. The investors are watching videos of financial professionals. Depending on whether or not they like what they are hearing, they "dial up" or "dial down" from the midpoint of a scale that goes from 0 to 100. First, they watch a video of a well-dressed man as he says the following:

What they do is combine statistical arbitrage with merger arbitrage, and they do currency draft trading as well as a little long, short, and global macro work. They seek to go away from the mainstream, to less efficient areas of the world, and really try to exploit inefficiencies in those markets using leverage.

Even though he then confidently describes how they earn money from this approach, and how they have several PhDs on their staff, the dials tell a different story—they drop all the way to zero. And the comments from the group are emphatic:

"I have a PhD degree, and I didn't understand a thing he said."

"He was trying to baffle us with BS."

"If we met at a cocktail party, I would have walked away by the third word."

Next, a second video shows another financial advisor who looks straight into the camera, and slowly and purposefully says the following:

Every portfolio strategy we create is customized to your particular situation. What might work for someone trying to save for their child's college tuition probably won't be the best plan for someone who never had kids and wants to retire early. We recognize this. That's exactly why we spend so much time and effort making sure your portfolio strategy is

right for you and no one else. Sure, it may mean more work on our end
that other firms might not think is necessary, but it's what makes your
portfolio strategy yours and no one else's.

This time the dials go straight up to nearly a perfect score of 100—
and in the discussion that follows, the panelists make it clear that they
feel that this person is building a partnership with them based on trust.

This example highlights the gap between what you say and what
people hear. While jargon and "expertise" chased people away from
even clear financial return, plainspoken language engaged everyone.

Communicating with clarity and simplicity is a foundation of
the language of trust. If people don't understand the advantages of
your mutual fund, the bill you are sponsoring in Congress, or the
product you are selling, you lose. Whether you are trying to gain
customers or get people to exercise more and eat their vegetables, you
need a simple, engaging argument to gain their attention *and* their
trust.

It may be easy to grasp this concept, but I have found that it is
much harder to execute it in practice. It is almost always easier to
write a good paragraph than a good sentence. And it is equally easier to use shorthand that you understand well rather than trying to
explain a complex concept in simple terms.

Here are three guidelines for using plain language to communicate better with your audience:

1. **People don't know what you think they know.** Chances are
   if you are trying to sell a product or an idea to someone else,
   you spend more time with that product or idea than with your
   audience. You think about it more and as a result you have a

more sophisticated understanding. Too often, we assume that our audience comes to the table with the same knowledge. But they don't. And the result is often a situation where the audience doesn't understand you but also doesn't want to admit it. Instead, they nod their head but don't buy what you are selling.

2. **Simple does not always mean short.** Too many people make this mistake. They try to simplify language by reducing the number of words. But simple just doesn't always mean short. It is always better to use five words to tell a clear story than use two and leave people confused.

3. **Say enough but not too much.** Sometimes the most effective way to build credibility and create an effective message is to stop talking. Too often communicators say too much. The key message gets lost, diminished, or overwhelmed by a negative message that should have been removed. Even if everything you say is in plain language, there is a point where too much plain language does more harm than good.

These guidelines form the component parts of a new clarity of thought, and of speech, that is essential to the language of trust. Put them to work, and you will not only be understood—you are much more likely to be believed.

People Don't Know What You Think They Know

If you are trying to sell a product or an idea, it is usually because you have a vested interest in it. You may work for the company that makes the product, or work with an organization trying to promote an idea. In either case, you almost always know more than the average person does about what you are selling.

The more time you spend in a company or with an organization, the more you develop and speak in a language that is unique to that group. Acronyms arise. Shorthand is developed. And sophisticated ideas are reduced to seemingly simple terms. Unfortunately, only the people who have been speaking the language understand what you mean. To create understanding—and then trust—you must translate what you know into language the uninitiated can understand. Here are three reasons why:

1. **We don't buy what we don't get.** Too many companies are doing a good job of communicating things in language we understand. They are simplifying complex concepts, and their sales improve as a result. Most consumers just don't have the patience to try to understand products or concepts that are overly complex. So they reject the hard-to-understand products in favor of the easy ones.

2. **We don't understand what you think we do.** We aren't stupid, but we don't remember anywhere near as much as we think. A famous study from the 1930s showed that students forget nearly 80 percent of the contents of a lecture within two weeks,

and more recent research shows that people remember the same words much less when they are in complex sentences.[10] Add to this the fact that we usually don't care as much about your product or your issue as you do and you can start to appreciate how much you need to simplify your approach.

3. **We don't pay as much attention.** According to scientists, our continuous attention span is often measured in seconds. And the late author Neil Postman makes the case that this attention span has been getting shorter over time; in his book *Amusing Ourselves to Death*, he blames a generation raised on television, and in an Internet era of instant access to information, this trend appears to be accelerating.[11]

On top of all of these trends is a world that is getting busier, and demographics that are trending older. These all add up to one thing: a consumer that has turned away from the acronym-laden, expertise-driven sales approach of a generation ago. Concepts will still need to be explained in the future, and people still need to be educated, but from here the world increasingly belongs to the clear and the simple.

There are many communicators out there who argue that they work in situations that require sophisticated terminology. In many cases, these people work in industries where there is an intermediary between them and the end beneficiary of a product. In health care, many companies communicate with the doctor, not the patient. In financial services, companies talk to the financial advisor, not the client. In employee benefits, they talk to the company's HR department, not the employees themselves. They claim that business-to-business audiences require sophisticated messages because they are sophisticated business customers. As a result they reject the need to translate their message into plain language. They are wrong for two reasons.

First, these communicators almost always overestimate the amount of knowledge that the audience has. Let me give you an example. We have worked with technology clients who assume all software developers and information technology pros closely follow emerging trends only to find they are completely focused on the technologies available to them today. These developers and IT pros may be aware of new trends in computing but they are certainly not sophisticated when it comes to talking about them. We have worked with rheumatoid arthritis patients who have suffered with the condition for years and still do not understand how it works or much of what their doctors say to them. We have worked with congressional staffers who make laws about the economy but don't understand economics. In each case, our clients have used sophisticated language to approach what they believed to be a sophisticated consumer. In each case, the language failed to persuade. More important, it tended to reinforce the audience's skepticism toward the company that was communicating.

Second, when the target audience is an intermediary—a financial advisor, HR person, doctor, etc.—the problem is compounded. Companies use sophisticated terms to talk to their clients (that is, the intermediaries) and then the intermediaries turn around and use the same language to their end clients. Even when this is explicitly not supposed to be the case, it happens every time. And it creates confusion and skepticism in the process. Instead, to build trust across the sales chain, you should always assume an unsophisticated listener. Talk at their level and you can build credibility with any customer.

Simple Does Not Always Mean Short

People often have misconceptions between clarity and brevity. The best example of this is text messaging today. For those who speak the language, simple is short. Why say in four words ("talk to you later") what you can say in four letters ("ttyl")? But for people who aren't used to text messaging, this shorthand is nonsense.

The same is true in business communications. Too often communicators use two words when they need five. For example, financial services professionals may talk about "longevity risk" when they should be talking about "ensuring that you have enough money as long as you live." Or worse, they start using acronyms like APV (adjusted present value) or GLWB (guaranteed lifetime withdrawal benefit) that, at best, put them one small step ahead of text messages.

Your message is a story. And in most cases, this story requires a narrative, not a shortcut. For people to hear your story, it needs to speak in their language of plain language, while connecting with their own lives.

Take the example of variable annuities. The basic definition of these investments in Wikipedia is as follows:

> A life annuity is a financial contract in the form of an insurance product according to which a seller (issuer)—typically a financial institution such as a life insurance company—makes a series of payments in the future to the buyer (annuitant) in exchange for the immediate payment of a lump sum (single-payment annuity) or a series of regular payments (regular-payment annuity), prior to the onset of the annuity.

Short? Yes. Technically correct? Yes. Engaging? No. For most people, this definition would only qualify as plain language if you worked for the IRS. Now, let's take a look at what we tell our clients about these investments:

We spend a lot of time talking to clients about the risks of retirement, but it's really time to talk about the opportunity of retirement. We live in an age where we have the opportunity . . . we have the likelihood that we're going to live ten, twenty, thirty, even more years in retirement. And we want, and we hope, that we can help our clients to take advantage of that opportunity.

Variable annuities can help your clients take advantage of this opportunity. It helps them to meet their retirement goals, to meet their life goals, by allowing them to invest less conservatively. Part of the cost of an annuity is to buy an insurance policy for your investments. As a result, annuities allow clients to invest more aggressively in investments that are likely to grow during their retirement period, without having to worry about what will happen if the market turns south. So instead of diversifying into a lower risk, lower reward investment, you can help them diversify with a higher reward, lower risk investment.

The second description has more than twice as many words as the first one. But it tells an engaging story about variable annuities, one that describes an investment that can grow with the market but has a guaranteed income benefit. It uses simple words that people can relate to more easily, even though it uses more of them.

Of course, simple can often mean shorter as well. Take the federal regulations that define the term "organic," which run over five hundred pages, and compare them with a popular definition of the term: only a bureaucrat will read the former. But for most things, simplicity and brevity do not necessarily go hand in hand. Think of how you might explain things to your fifth-grade child, and you are a good part of the way toward understanding how you should speak to everyone today.

Uncle Sam Wants You to Use Plain Language

Type the phrase "plain language" in Google and the first site it will return is from none other than the U.S. government: PlainLanguage.gov, an official site devoted to replacing bureaucratic prose with clear writing in Washington and beyond.

The site looks at the history of the plain language movement in the U.S. government (it's short, dating back to President Nixon in the 1970s), and weighs in with an extensive list of words not to use. Here are some examples, with suggested replacements:

Don't Use	Use
Adjacent to	Next to
Disseminate	Send
Expeditious	Fast
Heretofore	Until now
Notwithstanding	Still
Optimum	Best
Parameters	Limits
Remuneration	Payment
Subsequent	Next
The undersigned	I

Set aside in bold on this list are their "dirty dozen" of the worst words and phrases to use in English, such as: addressees, assistance, commence, implement, in accordance with, promulgate, and utilization. Even "it is" makes the list, with a recommendation that it be omitted entirely.

Across the Atlantic is the corresponding site PlainEnglish.co.uk, a private site spearheading a campaign that earned founder Chrissie Maher that country's Order of the British Empire award. In addition to examples and a word database, it also contains a web-based software program called DrivelDefence that will analyze your text or website for clarity. (A test using a generous sample of this chapter passed, by the way.)

Say Enough but Not Too Much

In our work, we often find that the single most effective way to use language to build trust is to use the delete key. It takes a great deal of the right language to build trust and just a few of the wrong words or messages to kill it. Similarly, you can take a great message that improves your credibility and lose it by wrapping it in too many other messages. Overcoming skepticism requires that you say the right things. It also demands that you remove the wrong things and not say too many things. The challenge: very often the wrong things for your audience are just the things that you most want to say. So successfully limiting your message often means losing some of the messages that matter most to you.

How many times have you looked at a newsletter, an email, or even a brochure and checked out how many pages you had to read before starting to read it? Or stopped reading something after the second paragraph because you were already bored, even though there might have been an important message in the document? Or heard someone criticized for saying in a hundred words what could have been said in ten? Now think about examples of CEOs, celebrities, or even children trying to explain why they don't deserve to be blamed for something they did. More often than not, their statement will be longer, there will be more "hemming and hawing," and the point of the response will often get lost in a sea of unnecessary words. And with every additional word, trust disappears a little more.

There are many ways people talk about this problem. In sales, people say "don't sell through the sale" because many salespeople have the habit of blowing things by failing to stop talking when the buyer has already demonstrated he or she is ready to buy. And the idea that "less is more" is often talked about but rarely followed. And there is a truism among communicators and copywriters that lazy writers are more verbose because it is almost always harder to clearly summarize a point in a sentence than it is to do so in a paragraph.

But the same idea is true in all cases: At some point, more words mean less understanding, lost attention, and a missed opportunity. And in the worst of cases, talking too much creates problems that the communications were designed to help avoid in the first place.

Probably the best example of this was the 2009 explanation and apology by Governor Mark Sanford of South Carolina about going missing from the state and having an extramarital affair. Governor Sanford was commonly cited as a likely presidential candidate before the scandal. After it, his own party tried to oust him from the governorship. The reason was less about the fact that he had an affair than in the way he apologized for his misdeeds.

What should have been limited to a short apology and explanation revealed far more information than was helpful for him. His initial apology was a rambling fifteen-hundred-plus-word confession. Then he kept the story in the news for days by expanding upon his apology in ways that can only be described as a little bit crazy. Then he went on to take specific questions about the affair from the press.

Then he released emails that included intimate details of his extramarital relationship and included Sanford confessing to feeling like a teenager and rhapsodizing over details like his mistress's tan lines.

This problem comes up in many situations. My firm has worked on a host of internal communications engagements for major companies. In every case, the company is trying to build credibility with its employees through better internal communications. In nearly every case, management has recognized that the message they are trying to communicate is not getting through. Often the substance of the message needs to be improved. But in many cases, the core of the problem is not the substance of the message but the fact that it is getting lost in too much communication.

Important messages are included in newsletters together with less important messages and get lost as a result. Or they are the third point in an employee email, and the readers never get down that far. Or the point is communicated in five paragraphs when it should be communicated in two. And there is the most common problem—information overload—where employees are so used to being bombarded with messages of mixed importance that they simply stop reading.

The answer: Internal communicators have to make a tough choice. They can say everything and find that little gets heard, or not say too much so that the messages they need to communicate actually get through.

Does this happen in your organization?

Another clear example is when companies are selling a product and they try to come up with every single argument or feature to list on the packaging or put in their messaging. Have you ever seen those packages that list fifteen features for their products? Do you think anyone ever makes a decision whether or not to buy something based on the fifteenth feature on the list? It doesn't happen.

In fact, we have worked on a number of messaging projects that specifically try to identify the right number of messages to use in a given campaign. Often we use a technique called total unduplicated reach and frequency (TURF) analysis, a research technique typically used for providing estimates of media or market potential. Without getting into the boring details, TURF helps you identify the best combination of messages to reach the most people with an argument that the audience finds effective. It also shows you the point of diminishing marginal returns when adding one more message will have little or no impact.

In our experience, there is rarely a case where you need more than five messages to reach your maximum audience. In many cases you get 90 percent of the way there with three messages. And there is no question that in the real world, your audience is more likely to listen to three arguments, features, or messages than five or seven.

When it comes to talking about more controversial issues, it becomes even more important not to say too much. For example, I recently worked with a pharmaceutical company that had just won a patent-protection suit against generic drug manufacturers. This company was in a situation where it was in the right, but consumers couldn't care less: the cost of their medicine was going to be higher, and the profitability of a drug manufacturer was not exactly top of mind with them.

The challenge was that the battle over the medicine's patent had been very emotional for the company. It had taken years and cost a tremendous amount of money and senior executive time. In the process, the company was forced to cut jobs and close facilities. The company had also lost sales and had been often attacked by critics and the competition for its stance. Now that the company had won its lawsuit, it wanted to convey all of these messages in its own defense. But in our testing, these statements actually hurt the company's message. According to one research participant, "It's like saying 'my pain is worse than your pain' and I'm not sympathetic to that." At the end of the day, much of this company's internal argument for protecting its patents went on the chopping block in their public statements.

Instead, we identified the messages that would be effective to communicate. We first found that there were three core messages to which consumers responded: that this was about a medicine designed to help people, produced by a small and dedicated company, and that this was a question of what was fair. In rough terms, the messages went like this:

> This issue is not about some abstract patent dispute. It is about a real medication that is prescribed to real patients to treat a serious health issue.
>
> We are a small specialized pharmaceutical company with a track record of balancing the needs of patients with the needs of our business.
>
> When several generic drug companies infringed our patents, we acted to protect our rights. Just because the generics companies didn't like the rules didn't mean they had the right to break them.

Patients responded to each of these elements. We knew the price of the medication was a serious issue for patients so we began with an acknowledgment that the company took it seriously as well (which it did). Emphasizing that this was a small, specialized company, versus giants like Merck or Bristol-Myers, was also important for connecting with people. Because there is so much mistrust of "big pharma" it was important to make it clear that this was not just one product from a huge portfolio; it was the company's lifeblood.

The bottom line? We found the right combination of messages to improve favorability of the company while eliminating the messages that didn't help our client to communicate its position. Our surveys showed the right messaging resulted in a 20 percent increase in favorability when the right messages were used.

Bringing this example around to your own communications, it means that the process of building a message that will be credible with your audience requires you to start with what matters most to your audience. Take all the reasons, rationales, and arguments for your message, and chop them mercilessly. Eliminate the messages that you want to say but that your audience doesn't want to hear. This doesn't mean you should hide things that are important to accurately assess the issue. Instead, it means eliminating any support points for your argument that are inconsistent with your audience's "truth." Keep cutting until you have a simple, clear, benefit-driven message that people remember—and anyone could repeat from memory. By adopting a "less is more" mantra, you harness our natural tendency to process and trust simple messages, and leverage it to your advantage.

5

Be Positive

The Positive Principle:
Negativity Breeds Contempt

Is your bathroom breeding Bolsheviks?

That is what one 1930s advertisement asked. As a scowling worker clutched an inferior paper towel, this ad equated poor restroom supplies with socialism and labor activism. And this toweling ad was not alone: pick up a newspaper from that era, and you will find ads with stern warnings about everything from body odor to unsanitary cigars.

Of course, you don't need to go back that far to see examples of using fear to sell products, policies, and ideas. From negative advertising in political campaigns, to scare tactics selling wars and economic policies, to insurance companies who warn people about leaving their family broke, we still see subtler versions of the same fear-based tactics used decades ago.

In fact, many of us are trained to use scare tactics and negative incentives to motivate people to act. And most of us who have been trained in fear-based selling are convinced it works.

But does it?

My firm's research—along with a careful analysis of how we buy today—shows that negative messages no longer work the way they did in the past. Rather than building trust between the communicator and the audience, negative messages push people away. On issue after issue and in industry after industry, we have seen the power of negative messaging to do damage to a client's objectives:

- Companies want to create a "need" in the marketplace so they try to instill fear. Yet rather than generating purchase interest, fear generates paralysis.

- Industries often respond to attacks from activists or politicians by "fighting back" and going after the credibility of the activists. But in most cases, the public rejects these responses as biased and the industry as guilty.

- Politicians try to win elections by frightening voters with stories of how bad things would be if their opponent gets elected. These scare tactics do add to the public's list of turnoffs—the things that turn them off from politics altogether.

The bottom line is that the language of fear in sales has outlived its relevance.

What Is Wrong with This Picture?

Money is a universal concern for retirees. So what is wrong with this typical sales pitch for a retirement investment?

> *We all hope that the market does well during our retirement. But what if you retire right at the beginning of a long bear market? In order to get the returns you want, you will have to leave your money in the market until it turns around. It could be two years or ten years. But until it turns, your quality of life in retirement, unfortunately, can suffer at the whim of the market.*
>
> *This investment can protect you against that risk. It can provide you with protection in the down years without limiting your ability to get performance in the good years.*

Every word of these statements is accurate. None of them are exaggerated. All of them can be backed up by years of financial statistics. So why does our consumer testing show that people get turned off when they hear this?

It's all in the words. Look a little more closely: "bear market," "suffer," "risk," "down years." "A market that could take as long as ten years to recover." Pretty grim, right?

The problem here isn't one of honesty. It is one of linguistics and culture. Americans don't buy fear. Why? Y2K, the bailouts, and just about every single infomercial. Fearmongers in the past didn't act in our best interest. Because of the people who told us we had better act today or else, many of us now equate fear-based selling with liars and cheaters.

Do we ever respond to fear? Of course. It is why most of us follow the speed limit, file our tax returns, and don't do drugs. But many people do not realize that the power of this fear as a motivating force has been on a steady but perceptible decline for many years: psychologists call this phenomenon *learned helplessness*, where we eventually stop responding to negative stimuli after we experience too many of them.

At a social level, fear has been long losing its power as a selling point. In our own research, we see in nearly every situation that positive words trigger a much more powerful call to action than negative ones. Moreover, negative words now often have a paradoxical effect on consumers: instead of motivating people, they turn them off, *no matter how correct they are.*

Don't believe us? Take a look in your pantry, refrigerator, closet, and medicine cabinet. Where you used to see packaging touting value and superiority over other products, a new trend exists: absence labeling—"hormone-free," "trans-fat free," "made without chemicals." Ten years ago, trans fat was barely on our radar. Most people still don't know what many of the things they want their products to be free of even are. With absence labeling, discounting the competition (those products that have hormones, trans fat, and/or chemicals) is implied. No attacks are necessary. Creating positive values without directly attacking your competitors through absence labeling is an everyday example of how companies are starting to get smart to the potential of being positive.

This flies in the face of the history of selling, particularly in the financial industry. For example, an insurance sales manual from the 1930s instructs salespeople to ensure that both the husband and the wife are present, and then turn to the wife and ask, "What would you do if your husband died unexpectedly?"

Today, things aren't always much different. David was recently at an insurance conference in Florida and heard one speaker warn of a "senior's ghetto" forming inland from the affluent beach dwellers who first started moving down in the 1970s, growing under the weight of people who haven't planned for retirement. When David challenged this assumption, the speaker literally stood on a table and bellowed that "If seniors don't get what we are talking about, and buy what we are selling, they will die broke and face financial ruin!"

The roots of negative selling run deep. It has a long history of success. But our culture has changed, and negative selling is no longer consistent with who we are as consumers. You aren't listening to that guy standing on the table anymore, and if that insurance salesperson from the 1930s showed up nowadays, you would tartly inform him who should be asking the questions. Yet salespeople still often find themselves in that gray area between creating fear and illustrating a need—which in turn costs them sales.

Today, the language of trust is built on a much more positive approach to communications. Here are some of its key principles:

1. **Positive is not Pollyanna.** Positive language works when it turns real facts into an optimistic or positive view of the world. For example, a few years ago Verizon turned around its reputation as a tired telephone company with the tagline "Making progress every day." The line was effective because it spoke in positive terms about the steps Verizon was taking to build a better business, without selling customers something that was too positive to be credible.

2. **Positive is forward-looking.** In a financial crisis, most investors don't want to dwell on how bad things were. Instead,

they want to spend most of their time and energy thinking about the future and how to make the most of their current situation. Likewise, customers wronged by a company don't want companies to spend their time explaining why problems occurred. Instead, they want to hear about what the company will do tomorrow to fix the situation.

3. **Positive is *for* things, not *against* them.** Too often salespeople and communicators spend their time talking about what is wrong with the status quo, the competition, or their critics and not enough time articulating their own value proposition. Fear-based selling is itself based on the idea that you need to focus on an "other"—that which creates fear—rather than the "self"—the reason to buy your product or idea.

    The same is true in politics, reputation management, and issue advocacy. For every moment that you spend trying to define the "other," it is critical that an even greater amount of time is spent on communicating your or your company's benefits. Even comparative advertising is increasingly sensitive to the way a company takes on its competition. For example, Apple can attack Microsoft because it uses a positive vehicle—humor. But try to directly attack a competitor in serious terms and your audience is likely to turn off or tune out.

All three of these principles join together to create speech that engages people—and in the best case, uplifts them and makes them part of something greater than themselves. Let's take a look at how to put each of them to work.

Different Words, Different Reactions

A group of priests once asked their superior if it would be okay to smoke while they prayed. "No, that would be sacrilegious!" replied the supervisor. Months later, and a little wiser, they went back to their superior again and asked if they could pray while they smoked. "Why yes, that would be wonderful!" was the reply this time.

Different words and phrases are often processed completely differently, even when they mean exactly the same thing. Psychologists call this process *reframing*, where an idea is expressed in more palatable terms to connect better with people. Invesco recently did a study comparing how consumers reacted to different phrases with identical meanings and found wildly different results for which phrases interested them more. In each case below, the term that uses "risk"—the negative—dramatically underperforms the alternative.

Making sure you can participate in the gains while
    reducing your downside risk ....63 percent
Managing market risk...37 percent

Making sure you can afford to maintain
    your lifestyle..81 percent
Managing inflation risk... 19 percent

Making sure you have enough money as
    long as you live...90 percent
Managing longevity risk... 10 percent

The lesson here is that ideas alone are not enough to communicate with customers: these ideas must be framed in a way that is as positive for the listener as possible.

Positive Is Not Pollyanna

Being positive has the vibe of being a personal virtue. It rolls off the tongue with the same kind of feeling as being nice, polite, or pleasant. But the term actually has a much more technical meaning for us: the dictionary defines it as "characterized by affirmation, addition, inclusion, or presence rather than negation, withholding, or absence." In other words, being positive is more than anything *a choice of words*.

What we are not saying is that you should go out with rose-colored glasses and attempt to convince skeptics that everything is positive. They won't buy it. What we are saying is that your language must be positive but not *too* positive. It must reflect the audience's view of the world without asking them to subscribe to something that they simply don't believe possible.

This difference between being positive and Pollyanna is discussed in much greater detail in the next chapter on plausibility, but it is worth raising here because I don't want you to get the wrong idea. Positive language means taking a glass-half-full approach to communicating. Don't tell people the glass is half empty. But also don't try to convince them that they are about to get a full glass of water.

Positive Is Forward-Looking

Be honest. When the markets are down, how quick are you to open your bank or brokerage statements? At the time we should perhaps pay the most attention to our finances, many of us simply tune out instead. The bills pile up. We would rather not confront the reality that we lost money.

Logic fails us when it comes to bad news. In 1990, when economic times were fairly good, there were ten personal investment magazines, replete with pictures of helicopters and fancy cars. By 2003, with a considerably tighter economy, only three of these magazines still existed. This is also counterintuitive. Didn't people technically need investment advice more in 2003?

Our feelings are emotional, not technical. Many people do not open their bank or brokerage statements when things are not going well in the market. We leave the credit card bill sitting on the counter when we are not feeling financially secure. And we often put off getting a physical if we fear that a health issue is looming. Yet marketers and salespeople often focus on the problems of today instead of the benefits for tomorrow. It's a mistake. If you want to build trust with customers, don't dwell on how bad their situation is now. Tell them how much better it will be as a result of your product or service (assuming this is true).

Words to Lose	Words to Use
Immediate	Long term
React to the market	Strategic

There are two magic words when it comes to talking about investing with many investors: long term and strategic. Even in the face of steep losses in their portfolios, most investors want to focus their time thinking about their long-term prospects. Even preretirees—those most likely to need short-term income—respond more favorably to the idea of investing long term than to a conversation focused on the short term. And when they talk with financial advisors, they want to hear about "strategies" because the idea of a strategy is both optimistic and forward-looking.

The same is true when companies try to use their own problems as a way to promote a policy or public opinion agenda. With the significant exception of those companies that successfully argued during the financial crisis that they were too big to fail, this approach never works. Put simply, no one cares about your business's issues and problems. No one wants to hear your bad news. They don't care why situations are a challenge for you. And they certainly don't want you to make your problems their problems. Talking to your customers about your problems puts you in the position of making excuses instead of finding answers—and this in turn knocks ten points off your credibility.

We proved this point recently when we were working with a major electric utility. This utility was asking for a steep rate increase at a time of rising demand and higher fuel costs, and was strategizing how to communicate this increase to the public.

Our job was to explain the increase in a way both residential and business customers would not necessarily like but accept. In other words, we had to appeal to the skeptics. The problem was that this utility—like many companies—preferred to speak in candid, negative terms. It tried to explain why higher costs to the utility were driving higher rates. It tried to demonstrate how a failure to increase rates would increase the possibility of bankruptcy for the utility. It tried to educate customers about how increasing reliance on energy-using appliances, computers, and other electronics had resulted in increased demand and, as a result, higher costs. And it focused on how actions in the past had created a situation that required more money from customers in the future.

Though every argument was true, each was rejected by customers. Customers felt that the utility had made bad decisions in the past, and now customers were forced to pay the price. They believed that the threat of bankruptcy was heavy-handed and signaled poor management. And they resented the implication that it was somehow the customers' fault that the utility had to build new capacity (in fact, they felt that the need for greater capacity is usually a sign that companies are making lots of money and should result in lower, not higher, rates).

In general, they didn't want to hear about a big corporation's problems—least of all one that was a monopoly and provided an essential service. As one participant put it, "We don't care about the woe is me, we care about the value added." So what did their customers value? The customers wanted to hear about the future. They wanted to know what they would get for the increased rates tomorrow instead of why yesterday's actions now created the need for this rate increase. They wanted to know that they would continue to get reliable service today and in the future and that the company was making the right investments in infrastructure and cleaner energy sources. Based on the results of our Instant Response testing, we drew up a blunt comparison for our client that read as follows:

- This rate case *is not* about your utility. It *is* about your customers.

- It *is not* about doomsday scenarios of what happens if your utility doesn't get the rate increase. It *is* about what you need to do to ensure reliable electricity for the future.

- It *is not* about bad credit ratings and poor profit margins. It *is* about ensuring the good financial health of your utility for the future.

- It *is not* about justifying the benefits of natural gas over the past decade. It *is* about the opportunities of smart investments in alternative energy for the future.

- It *is not* about the increased usage of your customers. It *is* about meeting the needs of all of your customers for the future.

- It *is not* about a single moment in time. It *is* about your utility's track record of good service and your commitment to investment and innovation.

- It *is not* about "us versus them." It *is* about "all of us working together."

The formula for taking this perspective and applying it to communication is fairly straightforward:

1. **Emphasize your company's commitment to customers.** Always start with what you deliver to your customers that they value most. Whether it is reliability, safety, quality, or variety, this is the place to start a positive message even if you have fundamentally bad news to deliver. This is a way to keep credibility by reminding your customers that you know what is important to them.

2. **Acknowledge the problem and your commitment to find a solution.** Recognize the issue on your audience's mind and outline a solution that works for your customers and your company. Never avoid acknowledging the problem. You know it is there. Your customers know it is there. Get it out in front of the conversation. We often communicate the anticipated solution as one that needs to balance competing needs (for example,

between access and innovation; between cost and reliability; between the needs of the environment and affordability).

3. **Talk about your role and responsibility.** If you need to ask the public or your customers for something they don't want to give, you had better tell them about all the actions you took to avoid having to make that request in the first place. You must take some responsibility before you ask your audience to participate.

4. **Talk about how you will avoid this problem again in the future.** As customers, we are often willing to allow companies to make a mistake once. But if they do it again, we will move on to the next company. So a big part of building credibility is talking about how you will change in the future to avoid a repeat of the past. Here, details and specifics are critical.

5. **Then make the request.** Only after taking all of these steps should you ask your customers or the public to make a sacrifice on your behalf.

When we test consumer reactions to bad news, they almost always react negatively to companies that talk about their own interests. Conversely, when you create positive messages that speak to the customers' interests, you have a much better chance of creating a dialogue where people understand and accept your message.

Put the Positive News First

As part of our work together, the four of us conduct WordLab workshops with marketing departments at leading insurance companies. These sessions are intensive four-hour workshops designed to tackle specific language and communication issues applying the language of trust. As one team of marketers reviewed their twenty-four-page brochure (brochures for variable annuities are never short) with respect to the Positive Principle, they discovered a major flaw in their materials. The words were not offensive, but the order was a problem. The first twelve pages of the brochure focused on problems investors faced in retirement. It was depressing.

By comparison, the last twelve pages of the brochure contained detailed information about products and solutions. It was very positive. It read very well. But the WordLab showed us what the problem was with it: *people never got there.* By following the traditional sales dictum to sell the problem first, and then the solution, they produced an expensive document that no one read past the negative. And until they tested it, they would have had no idea it was hurting them instead of helping them.

Positive Is *for* Things, Not *Against* Them

Republicans versus Democrats. Hatfields versus McCoys. Corporations versus activists. Everywhere from politics to popular culture, the urge to form partisan tribes seems to define society. Unfortunately, our research shows that giving rhetorical nods to these partisan urges is the kiss of death for anyone trying to market to the public, unless you are a political pundit or shock jock.

*   *   *

Does this mean that you have to start walking arm in arm with the people who ideologically oppose you? Basically, yes. In a world of skeptics, you can't only be against others anymore: you have to be *for* something. And lack of credibility now demands that when an opponent lobs an issue at you, you do more than defend yourself—you must now acknowledge it and shake their hand.

From lead in lipstick to hormones in milk, my firm has conducted research to test the way industries and companies should respond in the face of attacks from activist groups. In general, conflicts between an industry and its critics have tended to become propaganda wars with dueling websites, advertisements, and spokespeople. Each side spins the facts in their favor and tries to convince the public they are right. And our research shows that the public's reaction could be summed up as "a pox on both your houses."

My research with consumers has repeatedly found that messages that directly attack the credibility of activist groups are viewed negatively by the public. Rather than undermining the critics, these self-serving attacks tend to be dismissed as biased responses that deserve little respect. Answering attacks in this way merely validates them in the eyes of your audience.

The activist group's message is fairly straightforward. They release studies claiming to demonstrate that an industry's products cause cancer or some other condition. And the response from industry is usually a blanket defense of their product's safety and an attack on the critics for things like "junk science" or "biased research."

Rather than listening to industry's arguments, the public responds by assuming that the industry's strong defense is almost an admission of guilt. In a fight between two antagonists, both are considered too extreme. Neither has the credibility to truly persuade. What the public wants is an unbiased view of the situation. They want information and the ability to judge for themselves the right answer. Here is one positive message that resonated with our research participants.

> We both want the same thing—to provide the public with the information they need to make the most informed choices about the products they purchase for themselves and their families. The fact that we're both so committed about this issue is good news for the American public.

This response was not just words, but part of a strategy that focused on transparency rather than self-interest, including the development of online resources for consumers to help them make up their own minds.

What you are seeing here is part of a larger trend we see in credibility: the folly of vilifying others who disagree with you. Rather than strengthening your position, this approach almost always backfires. Here are some examples of words to use when people challenge you. Note carefully that we are not asking you to agree with the other party. We are simply asking you to stop trying to win your battles through character assassination, and start winning by creating credibility. Compare these phrases and see what we mean:

Negative Response	Positive Response
Our opponents have an extremist agenda.	There are certain things we can all agree on …
Their facts are distorted.	Their facts raise important points. Here is some additional information.

Negative Response	Positive Response
They are biased and have no credibility.	They have one of many views on this situation.
They are standing in the way of progress.	They represent people who understandably feel cautious about this.
They will never be satisfied.	They have significant reservations.

What you are seeing here is not reverse psychology: it is aligning yourself with reality. The argument for a positive stance—even with critics with whom you strongly disagree—lies not only in a mind-set of creating trust but an understanding of how people respond to self-defense:

- Defensive messages make you a partisan of your own interests, not your customers'.

- Defensive messages put you in a one-down position, while positive ones make you equal or superior.

- Defensive messages provoke further response from the other side, while positive ones defuse them.

Listen to most political disagreements on television, where spokespeople for opposing viewpoints attack and undermine each other, and you will see exactly what our research shows: you generally lose respect for the attacker, *even when you agree with his or her view.*

Most people believe that most serious issues are more complex than the media would suggest today. They deal with issues in their own lives where they must make trade-offs and balance competing interests. They understand that the same is true with larger issues as well. When parties take extreme views, it forces people to choose between black and white. If you happen to be closer to their view to begin with, then this approach will help you keep them on your side. But if they don't agree with you to begin with (remember we are talking about selling to skeptics here), then extreme arguments push them away from you.

Alternatively, when someone gives the other person credence, we tend to listen more carefully to what they have to say. Put another way, most spokespeople defend their views in a way that would never work in an argument with their spouse at home—and increasingly won't work with the public either.

This is where using positive words stops being sunshine and flowers, and starts becoming part of the hard work of generating credibility and trust. The Biblical injunction to love your enemies is no longer just a prescription for virtue. Research shows that it holds the key to good communication, conflict resolution, and consensus as well.

The 2008 Presidential Election: The Death of the Negative Campaign?

No matter what your political persuasion, one thing has been a truism for decades in major U.S. elections: negativity is powerful.

In 1964, a famous ad showed a little girl picking the petals off a daisy as a nuclear explosion erupts in the background, ending with an announcer gravely intoning, "Vote for President Johnson on November 3rd. The stakes are too high for you to stay home." By implying that

Republican challenger Barry Goldwater might be more likely to lead the country into nuclear war—an emotional rather than factual argument—Johnson helped seal a landslide victory.

In 1988, an issue that had nothing to do with federal policy—allowing weekend furloughs for convicted felons—was personalized in the form of Willie Horton, a convicted murderer who raped a woman after being furloughed, in ads against Democrat Michael Dukakis. Republican campaign manager Lee Atwater famously noted, "We're going to make (Horton) his running mate." And while Dukakis was merely supporting the longtime state policy of his predecessor, these ads played a role in his defeat.

As successful as these negative campaigns were in past electrons, many pundits feel 2008 was the year that negative campaigning fell on its face. It failed Democratic hopeful Hillary Clinton, who tried to raise the image of who needs to be in office when the phone rings at 3 a.m. with a crisis. It also failed Republican nominee John McCain, who hammered unsuccessfully at opponent Barack Obama's character and personal associations: in fact, such charges were derided as "swift boating," a pejorative term taken from the 2004 campaign's attack ads on John Kerry's military record by the group Swift Boat Veterans for Truth.

There are times when the damage done to the victim of a negative campaign is greater: because politics is a zero-sum game, you can sometimes afford to hurt yourself, as long as you hurt the other guy more. But this wasn't true in 2008. As *Washington Post* writer Michael Shear noted, the use of such tactics now often "angers swing voters, who often say they are looking for candidates who offer a positive message about what they will do . . . (especially) this year, when frustration with Washington politics is acute and a desire for specifics on how to fix the economy and fight the wars in Iraq and Afghanistan is strong."

Even a decade ago, research was showing that negative campaigning was losing its effectiveness. According to a 1998 University of Missouri study, only 21.9 percent of people saw negative campaign ads as informative, and just 13.5 percent found them to be truthful. Meanwhile nearly 60 percent got a more negative impression of both the sponsor and the target. So even as laws have made it easier for groups such as political action committees (PACs) to create such ads in recent years, their effectiveness is diminishing.[12]

Back to Our Positive Roots

If negative selling goes back decades or even centuries, why are people suddenly exhausted by it in the early twenty-first century?

Part of it is a culture change. Mass media has, in a very real sense, taken over the role of spreading fear from salespeople. In fact, the media have done too good a job. In the media, there's no doubt that negative messages draw viewers and readers. The difference? Media outlets are not using the negative message to sell their own products. In other words, no news outlet tries to scare people into watching or reading its news; instead, the scaring is the news. So, we might all instinctively watch the car-crash video, but that doesn't mean it is an effective video to use to sell cars.

Today's consumers grew up bombarded by messages, most of them negative, for much of their waking hours. After a while, individuals and entire societies simply become desensitized. Or worse, they have come to resent those who try to scare them into a decision about what to purchase or for whom to vote.

Rotary International is a global service organization that was founded over a century ago with a guiding principle of what they call the "four-way test," which governs what its members say to people:

- Is it the TRUTH?

- Is it FAIR to all concerned?

- Will it build GOODWILL and BETTER FRIENDSHIPS?

- Will it be BENEFICIAL to all concerned?

Communicators need to develop their own four-way test—one that not only addresses the issues of equity and fellowship listed previously, but focuses our language toward the aspirational goals of the audience. As you should know by now, it all starts with the words we use.

We all know words create emotion. The key to creating trust is using the emotional impact of our words as a strategic advantage.

6

Be Plausible

The Plausibility Principle: Life Isn't Perfect; Neither Is What You Are Selling

It should be no surprise that your audience questions your intentions when you try to sell them an idea or a product. After all, companies and politicians and marketers of all sorts have long made promises they couldn't keep and made claims that didn't hold water. You are simply suffering the consequences of all of those liberties that others have taken with language. And now you face a credibility gap—the disconnect between what you say and what your audience believes.

Each of the previous chapters has outlined a piece of the overall approach that we believe is necessary to close that gap. Those chapters set the stage. Personalizing the story lets people know that you are paying attention to them. Using plain language demonstrates that you want them to understand what you are selling. And being positive signals that you want to advocate for their interests rather than scare them into a decision. Each of these is essential to building trust. But this chapter focuses on the core of your sales pitch itself. Put simply, the best sales pitch or line of argument will fail if your audience rejects it as lacking credibility.

Your parents and teachers probably told you to always tell the truth. And then you went into business and learned another lesson, spoken or unspoken: exaggerate the benefits of what you are selling, or lose ground to those who do. For centuries, this approach worked. In the late 1800s, Coca-Cola claimed it could cure morphine addiction, neurasthenia, and impotence.[13] In the 1950s, the makers of Carter's Little Liver Pills were forced to change its name after it was discovered that they did nothing for the liver. And just a few years ago, several diet drug manufacturers were fined $25 million for false claims about weight loss.[14]

Somewhere between the outrageous claims of a century ago and the implied promises of today's products and services lies a massive social change: we learned that if things sound too good to be true, they probably are. The sale's superlatives of "best," "most," "guaranteed," and "lowest" don't tempt us anymore. Rather than capturing our attention and interest, these overstated promises only increase our skepticism.

As a result, it is no longer enough to simply sell your product based on the benefits. Today, products have to offer a clear benefit to customers *and* customers have to believe that the benefit is real. As a result, being plausible in our speech is now a ticket-of-entry skill for creating a relationship with customers or making a persuasive argument.

Plausible speech flies in the face of everything we have learned about human persuasion. Most of us are trained to sell benefits, overcome objections, and denigrate competitors. But in test after test, we find that all of these approaches are about as credible as a $25 street-bought Rolex. The language of trust demands that you rise above your own interests, each and every time you open your mouth.

Why Sincerity Is the New Black

Being plausible is much more than a good communications skill. It has become part of a fundamental shift in our culture—one that we will probably never turn back from in our lifetime.

Look at popular culture. Generations ago, in the shadow of two world wars, we gave birth to a generation of superheroes. These superheroes had weaknesses, but they didn't generally have flaws. Today's versions of those same superheroes have lost the veneer of perfection. It is their dark side that interests us; their inner demons that make the movies interesting. We reject the idea that even our superheroes can be perfect because we know that nothing that says it is perfect ever is.

Television sitcoms followed the same trajectory. In the 1950s, sitcoms portrayed families trying to outdo each other with better homes, cars, and clothes. Over the last decade, every single one of the top-rated and most critically acclaimed sitcoms has been about dysfunctional families. From *Family Guy* to *Everybody Loves Raymond* to *Arrested Development*, we watch these imperfect families because they better reflect what we know to be true about the world.

The same now must hold true in how we sell ideas. In a world of skeptics, we can no longer put the cart of sales before the horse of credibility. It starts with the words we use, but this is not just a change of language: it is a change of heart and mind that consumers expect. The truth isn't spoken. It's heard.

The hardest part about creating plausible messages is that they are often confused with weakness. Rather than making bold statements, plausible messages will include intentional caveats. Rather than allowing no room for disagreement, plausible messages will acknowledge other opinions. And rather than claiming perfection, plausible language acknowledges flaws. By these measures, plausible messaging is weaker than traditional marketing messaging. But it is also more believable. So you can have a strong message that is rejected in disbelief or a weaker message that is trusted for its honesty and transparency.

Here are three keys to creating plausible messages.

1. **Plausible language is neutral.** When I do Instant Response testing with today's consumers, the response is highly predictable: self-congratulation gets dialed down, and authentic information gets dialed up. Companies like State Farm are more trusted by the public because they don't say that "State Farm is great," they say "State Farm is *there*." Plausible messages don't tell the audience what to think; they focus on providing the right information skeptics need to make up their minds in a way that favors the communicator.

2. **Plausible language is complete.** What is the best way to get people to believe in your product? Talk about the pros *and* the cons of it. That is why products like Great Britain's Marmite, a yeast spread with an acquired taste, achieved renewed popularity with the slogan "You love it or you hate it." Lines that make it clear that a product is "not for everyone" or that highlight the limitations of an argument (for example, "Yes, this

will result in somewhat higher costs, but it will also . . .") build credibility by offering the complete picture.

3. **Plausible language avoids superlatives.** Remember Crazy Eddie, the defunct 1980s electronics chain whose hyper-kinetic pitchman breathlessly declared that his prices were "i-n-s-a-a-a-n-e!"? Compare this with ads today for modern competitors like Best Buy and decide for yourself how marketing communication has evolved.

Let's look at each of these ideas in detail, and see how you can create a new sense of credibility with your own audience.

Plausible Language Is Neutral

Turn on cable news today and the last thing you will find is any evidence of neutrality. Fox News is blatantly conservative—and Fox News fans love the passion. MSNBC is equally liberal (or progressive depending on your preferred term) and their audience loves it as well. They each use extreme language to sell their own product. But they don't have to overcome skepticism to sell their product—their audience already agrees with them. Rather than looking to be persuaded, each network's audience wants to hear the latest highly partisan viewpoints to fuel their existing perceptions and give them ammunition for their next water cooler conversation.

For most everyone else, the job is not so easy. We are selling products or ideas to people who we must convince of the merits of our offering. Try to tell someone that you have the "best" product on the market and watch them reject you on the spot. Or talk to them about your "state-of-the-art" technology, "best-in-class" service or "proprietary" approach, and they will likely ignore the statements entirely. These statements don't work because they lack the requisite neutrality. They try to convince the audience of the merits without making a rational argument. And they fail because they suggest an inherent bias that ruins the integrity of the communicator.

We aren't just playing with words here, but replacing imputed judgments with rational arguments. Rather than trying to tell people what to think, give them the information they need to make the decision themselves. In the process we gain their trust and—assuming our product is as good as we believed it was—we will also get the sale.

So how do we know our language is neutral?

Neutral statements replace judgments with factual statements. Most of us speak in terms of judgments and conclusions: products are "great," people are "misguided," and of course our position is "right."

In reality, all of these words are illusions—and more to the point, they turn people off. "Great" means nothing today, in a world where different people have wildly different perceptions, and the same is true with "misguided" or "right": when was the last time someone got out of bed and said, "I'm going to be misguided and wrong today"? Today's consumer wants to hear your arguments and details so that they can draw their own conclusions—and according to our research will resist furiously any attempt from you to dictate them.

Neutral statements give details. No one wants to hear an endless list of features from you, but plausible speech tends to be longer on information and shorter on hyperbole. If your mind-set is to educate and clarify, and not simply to sell, you will find that your speech moves toward the right level of detail, sharing data that people want to hear. What is the right level of detail? Enough for thinking people to make up their minds about issues they care about without boring them and enough of the most pertinent information up front to satisfy most people. As we said in the chapter on being plainspoken, start with what matters most and stop when you think your customer will stop reading.

Pulling all of these components together, what you end up with is a way of speaking that is already familiar to all of us: namely, the voice and mind-set of someone who is knowledgeable, engaged, and nonpartisan. When you take on this voice within your own organization, you tap into the sincerity and objectivity that people now expect from everyone they deal with.

Words to Lose and Words to Use

Words to Lose	Words to Use
Dream retirement	Comfortable retirement

Ask people whether their top priority is a "dream retirement" or a "comfortable" one and the answer may surprise you. By more than six to one, Americans want a comfortable retirement over the dream. Why? Because the dream is just that—an implausible dream. When they think about retirement, they want something they can actually achieve—so it is much more credible to talk about a comfortable retirement.

Words to Lose	Words to Use
Guarantee	Protection
Financial freedom	Financial security

You would think that people would welcome strong words like "guarantee"—but in our consumer research, they don't. Too many people have seen guarantees fall prey to loopholes, business failures, or fine print. Protection is a somewhat weaker promise (it isn't a guarantee after all), but it is perceived as something a company can actually deliver on. "Financial freedom" is rejected because most Americans see freedom as a state where they have so much money they can do whatever they want. They also see this as incredibly unlikely. What is possible and is what they hope for is a future in which they have "financial security," or freedom from fear about their finances.

Words to Lose	Words to Use
Total	Portion
One-Stop	Diversified

People have become so used to the sales mentality that they often make assumptions that actually make it harder to sell a product. In the case of financial services, most investors subscribe to the cardinal rule of "don't put all your eggs in one basket." What is interesting is that, absent an explicit statement that an investment is only part of a larger diversification strategy, investors will assume the opposite. So communicating the word "portion" became essential to getting purchase consideration.

Words to Lose	Words to Use
World-Class, Leading	Comprehensive
Best of breed	Effective

More than anything, the PTE has ushered in the death of self-congratulatory prose. Once upon a time words like these conveyed superiority; today, they are trite, overused, and have lost their impact. Worse, they carry the baggage of all who came before you who never lived up to the commitment of these words. If you want to use descriptors, they need to be words that you can explain and, more important, back up with reasons.

Plausible Language Is Complete

Progressive Insurance understands the power of telling the whole story. Their business has been built on the idea that they will tell potential customers exactly what the competition is charging on their own website. In doing so, they give people a reason to check with Progressive first. They make it so that people don't feel like they have to go anyplace else. And most important, they build a huge degree of credibility by giving people information and then putting the power in the people's hands to make the right choice themselves.

In a world where the public believes that companies, politicians, salespeople, and other communicators are out to manipulate perceptions with language and messages, one of the most effective ways to build credibility—and achieve your objective—is to tell the whole story, not just your side of the story.

When a salesperson tells a prospect that "This product is not for everyone: here are the benefits, and here are the drawbacks," you gain much more credibility than saying, "Here is why this product is right for you." And ironically, the people who eventually purchase usually have a much stronger buy-in, once you provide all the facts.

Obviously, this won't work for everyone. If you sell an inferior product or believe that you need to hide information from your audience in order to achieve your objectives, then giving people both sides of the story won't help you. But if you believe that your product or idea can win in a fair fight, then being the source of the most complete information is a huge credibility builder.

You Can't See It or Say It, but It's There

Most people can't even pronounce the word "phthalates." It looks and sounds scary as it rolls off the tongue. And it has become a hot topic of concern in the personal care industry in recent years, as advocacy groups have raised issues about the long-term carcinogenic effects of these solubilizing agents in compounds such as cosmetics and fragrances.

So how does the personal care industry address these concerns? Not by taking a position on issues that have yet to be resolved at a regulatory level, but rather by opening up its standards and data to the public. In 2007 the Personal Care Products Council (PCPC), an industry trade group, released a Consumer Commitment Code that spelled out detailed guidelines for reporting adverse events, the maintenance of safety information, and the tracking of issues at a product level with the FDA.

Their website (cosmeticsinfo.org) shares a comprehensive database with consumers as part of this code, including extensive information on topics such as phthalates, as well as what forms of the chemical have been dropped from products recently based on current evidence, what forms are still in use, and links to current federal guidelines. Notably, it does not take a position on the use of these chemicals, but simply provides data.

Unlike many industries that wage propaganda wars with advocacy groups, organizations like PCPC serve as an example of a new approach for a new era: focusing on long-term product safety, and sharing information from objective sources in as much detail as possible.

From a communications perspective, the personal care industry's messages about the safety of its products are much more likely to be perceived as credible after being placed in the context of complete information.

Plausible Language
Avoids Superlatives

If you sell a credit card, how can you send consumers running for the exits? By offering it to them for "free." According to my firm's research, over 85 percent of affluent Americans would prefer a credit card with "no annual fee" than one that is "free," even though they mean exactly the same thing. Why? We have grown to suspect anything that sounds too good to be true—or even too good, period. It is plausible to be offered a card with "no annual fee." But most people simply reject the idea that a credit card would be completely free.

This example highlights the importance of getting the language right and the risks of using language that people reject as implausible. In the case of the credit cards, the issuer believed it had a great selling point ("it's free!"). What it found was that it ran the risk of turning high-value prospects against them by going overboard.

And this is not an isolated example.

We no longer believe in the language of absolutes—of black and white. Politicians and companies like to think that their audience thinks in these terms, but most people simply don't. Yes, on political issues there is 20 percent on each side of the issue that does see things in stark terms. The rest see varying shades of gray, and they expect people trying to persuade them to recognize the same reality. To these people—who make up most of the population—if you speak in absolutes you lose credibility. To be credible, you need to walk the line between brash and weak, and find messaging that is confident, convincing, and credible.

For example, I recently worked with a major energy company. It is a leader in biofuels and was trying to gain support for a decision to invest more money in an existing and much criticized technology. Except there were two problems: When it used its leadership as an argument for support, the public universally perceived it as arrogant and self-serving. Worse, because they perceived the company as arrogant, they also viewed the company's technology with even greater skepticism.

So my firm worked with the company to identify what messages would build credibility with the target audience. Rather than using superlatives and making bold claims, the public wanted humility, compromise, and self-reflection. Here are some of the public statements it started to look at:

> One of the keys to finding new solutions to our energy problems is through **partnerships** that bring together industry, government, and the world's best and brightest scientific minds to meet this challenge head-on. **No one company** can fix this problem alone. No one country can either.
>
> We have a unique opportunity in our history to **come together** and work as one to break our dependence on oil and limit its threat to our environment. **We know biofuels aren't perfect right now,** but we know with **more investment and more research** we can **continue** to refine our process so that the benefits of biofuels down the road will far outweigh the initial costs biofuels research incurs.

The words chosen here are all designed quite intentionally to drive credibility. I have bolded the key words. Here is why they were used:

- **"Partnerships"/"come together."** When it comes to solving big problems, the public feels strongly that partnerships are much more likely to succeed than individuals. By tapping into the "best and brightest scientific minds" (you can use superlatives when talking about other people!), this company is focused on getting to the right answer whether or not it does it themselves. The public is much more likely to believe that a group of organizations will figure out a solution than that a single organization can do so.

- **"No one company."** Here our client is purposely limiting expectations. Rather than making bold promises about the great challenges that it will overcome on its own, it is saying that it can only be part of the solution. That it will play its role, but others are needed. This language is not only humble; it increases the credibility of the communicator.

- **"We know biofuels aren't perfect right now."** Here is an example of acknowledging weakness. In this case, there are so many critics of existing types of biofuels that it was necessary to be open about the downsides of the technology it is talking about. By getting on the same side of the line as their critics, the company created an opening to take the conversation further and talk about the reasons for continued investment in this imperfect technology.

- **"More investment and more research"/"continue."** These phrases emphasize that building better technologies is a process— that it will take work and resources—and that the company is committed to that effort. This is an example of forward-looking language that demonstrates that the company is not happy with the status quo.

What is missing from all of this is a direct request for support for its continued investment. The company does get to that and it is well received, because it has built credibility for its position. Had it started with the sales pitch, it likely would have generated much more skepticism and a negative backlash.

Can You Be Plausible and Promotional at the Same Time?

Tooting your own horn with superlatives tends to make people shut down and not listen to you. But does that mean you can't ever bring yourself up? The answer is no—as long as you focus on what benefits the other person.

In the early days of the 2008 presidential election, one of its most well-received campaign spots came from former New York Mayor Rudolph Giuliani, as he painted a picture of what New York City was like before and after his tenure.

> New York City has been the third or fourth largest government in the country. It is one of the largest economies in the United States. They used to call it unmanageable and ungovernable. A large majority of New Yorkers wanted to leave and live somewhere else. It was a city that was in financial crisis, a city that was the crime capital of America, a city that was the welfare capital of America . . . a city that was in very difficult condition when I became the mayor.
>
> By the time I left office, New York City was being proclaimed as the best example of conservative government in the country. We turned it into the safest large city in America, the welfare-to-work capital of America, and most important, the spirit of the people of the city had changed. Instead of being hopeless, a large majority of people had hope. So I believe I have been tested in a way in which the American people can look to me. They are not going to find perfection, but they are going to

find someone who has dealt with crisis, almost on a regular basis, and
has had results—and in many cases, exceptional results, results people
thought that weren't possible.[15]

While Giuliani's candidacy was unsuccessful, this ad was one of the most highly rated in voter testing, including a rating of nearly 90 out of 100 from the moderate Republicans for whom the campaign was targeted. Why? Because he combined a vision of a better New York, an informational list of facts, and the humility to say he wasn't perfect, all in one neat package.

A New World of Plausibility

Will we ever see a world where an ad for a new truck says "this vehicle uses twice as much fuel as most passenger cars, but can transport heavy loads"? Or a politician says, "I plan to raise your taxes so we can improve social programs"? Or a concert is billed as "too loud for most people over twenty-one"? (Although the Heart Attack Grill in Chandler, Arizona, advertises on the door "The food you are about to consume is not healthy" and offers selections like the "quadruple bypass burger.")

We do not know if the gap between marketing and objectivity will ever be permanently closed, but we do know this much: it is going to get a lot smaller than it has been in past generations. Our consumers are often smarter than we are, and in our experience they are voting with their dial readings—and more often than you realize, with their feet. This means that plausibility is quickly becoming the new selling point of choice.

The language of plausibility is as close as our own experience. It simply involves taking on a new voice: not that of a partisan, nor that of an adversary, but of an engaged neutral observer. And ironically, it involves much less effort than our old efforts to spin everything. We just need to tell the truth in detail, like our parents and teachers once told us to.

Using the mechanics of plausible speech will help you adopt this voice quickly and more effectively. In the process, you will stand out in a marketplace where people still try much too hard to stand out. More important, you will build a relationship with people at a level that most people who sell products or ideas never get to see—standing eye to eye with them.

PART THREE

THE NEW WORD ORDER

When was the last time someone changed your mind? I don't mean persuading you of something you already believed in. I mean an opinion transplant.

It isn't easy to get skeptics to change their mind about you and what you are trying to sell. We've already discussed the four most important messaging principles for building trust with a skeptical audience—be positive, be plainspoken, be plausible, be personal. By considering each of these principles in your communication, you will get more people to listen to what you have to say. But wait, there's more! In fact, getting the messages right is only half the battle. If you start selling your product too early, or fail to place the messages in the appropriate context, the right messages will still fail. What we have learned in all of our research is that there is a process—a strategy—for communicating the right messages at the right time and in the right way to inspire trust in your audience. That is what the following section of this book is about.

Below is a graphic illustration of what we call the new word order—largely because it is built on the premise that the order of your communication is critical to your ability to engage skeptics. We've used a pyramid to represent the idea that each part builds on the one before it. The process is fairly linear, where you move from one step to the next in a sequence.

In the PTE, the most important first step in every selling conversation is engagement. If the skeptic isn't willing to listen to what you have to say, then even your best arguments will fail. So the first step is to find a way to engage someone who has little desire to hear what you have to say. This means finding a common area of agreement. So rather than starting a discussion by saying, "We need universal health care in America," you might start by saying, "We should get more for our money—we spend more money on health care in America than in any other country and don't have the results to show for it." Whichever side of the issue you are on, you will probably agree with that latter statement. And now that you agree on something, the audience is more likely to listen to what you say next.

After engagement, you can start the discussion. If you're trying to sell to a skeptic, the next step is to give her a reason to believe that you are going to do something other than simply argue your position or blindly sell your product. Because skeptics generally reject the idea that there is any perfect product or perfect solution to an issue, this next step is where you acknowledge their concerns right up front. It is where you demonstrate that the goal of the discussion is to promote the audience's interests rather than your own. So, continuing with our health care example, rather than saying, "We need to expand government assistance for health care so people can get the medical treatment they need," you could say, "Really, when you think about it, people like you and me end up paying so much more in taxes to cover emergency room costs that we wouldn't have to pay if everyone simply had access to a doctor before it was too late." In this case, you're not making it about the people who don't have health care, you're making it about the person you're talking to—and why she should care about reform because it could mean lower taxes for her.

So now that you've got her listening and you've framed the discussion around what's in it for her, you can start to sell your, well, whatever. This is the point where you pivot the conversation to your solution, your product, or your idea. But you can only make this shift once you've really gotten the listener engaged, and she understands that the issue is really about what's in it for her and why she should care. Once you've done that, you can start setting up the context for presenting the specifics of your plan. This step, which is so crucial, is the one most people fail to complete. More often communicators assume that they've gotten this far, so closing the deal will be a breeze once the facts are out on the table.

Wrong. Wrong. Wrong.

You can't forget, you're selling to a skeptic in the PTE . . . and they know that, too. Adjust for mistrust. So the minute you make the shift, their antennae will perk up as they ready themselves to say, "No, thank you." It's like an instinct they literally have to fight—the way you hold back a sneeze in the middle of an important meeting. Context is the crucial step that lays the groundwork for them to understand *why* what you're selling will actually help solve the problem *and* be in their interests, too.

Going back to our health care discussion, let's say you have a plan that's going to insure every single American and it's going to cost $100 billion to do so (this is only one-tenth of what many plans in 2009 proposed for health care reform). Still, that's a lot of money . . . even for Washington. Your skeptic probably isn't going to buy it. That's just too much money for our government to be spending at a time when we're still fighting two wars and our economy has taken a huge hit.

But what if you put that number in context? What if you were to also show the skeptic that Americans spend about $80 billion every year on cigarettes! That's not a misprint. Americans spend more on cigarettes in one year than any other country in the world spends on their military. And what if you went further to explain that, with only somewhat more than we spend on cigarettes every year, we could insure a population the size of Canada—the number of Americans who don't have access to affordable health insurance.

Now I can't guarantee this is going to win over your skeptic, but it's a start. Rarely do we change someone's mind *and* get that person to join the choir in a single sitting. But it's a way of having a discussion that isn't combative, defensive, or hostile. He may not jump on board for health care reform tomorrow, but he'll probably think about it a little bit harder. He might want to go out and find more information. And, in the end, he just might end up supporting your cause, or buying your product, whatever the case may be.

In the chapters that follow, I'm going to break down each of these three steps in the new word order to help you understand just how each one works. I'll explain the different approaches within each one, and show you how to put together an argument that even the most ardent skeptic would want to hear. Of course, depending on your audience, you may find yourself interchanging the parts of the pyramid to engage someone, but the direction remains the same. Even if you start with specifics as a way of engagement, you're still starting with engagement and moving on from there. You may also find yourself skipping engagement and going directly into making your argument relevant to your audience, but that's a judgment you'll have to make on a case-by-case basis. The overall approach will still apply.

7

Getting to Listen:
Engagement Before
Discussion

Are you really listening . . . or are you
just waiting for your turn to talk?

—Robert Montgomery

Sean Hannity doesn't convince anyone of anything; neither does Keith Olbermann. Every weeknight, these two men climb atop their electronic soapboxes and do the same thing over and over again: tell their audience exactly what they want to hear. They have guests on who almost always agree with what they have to say, or they bring guests on who disagree simply to show how quickly they can shout them down. They are echo chamber communicators who don't seek to persuade as much as they seek to incite.

Like so many in the blogosphere, they preach to their choirs and arm their followers with a litany of arguments to bolster positions with which the audience already agrees. That doesn't mean they don't have influence. They do. They have millions of followers (actually, Hannity has many more than Olbermann) who faithfully go around repeating their talking points ad nauseam. But they are selling to people who already believe. They are selling to people who trust what they have to say and look to them for guidance.

You should be so lucky. Selling to a world of skeptics is a much harder job.

Researchers at the University of Illinois and the University of Florida recently released research based on data from ninety-one studies involving nearly eight thousand participants. Their key findings: Most people seek out information that is already consistent with what they believe, filtering out the rest.[16] This is especially true on issues related to religion and politics, but it holds across the broad array of topics and issues people communicate about on a regular basis. The examples are everywhere. Think about the last time you were actually convinced to change your perspective on something about which you already had an opinion. Was it today, this week, this year? Chances are the examples of situations where you found information to support your point of view are much more common than situations that you truly approached with an open mind.

I see this concept, known as "confirmation bias," every day in my work. I see it with clients and with the thousands of members of the public with whom I speak during focus groups and Instant Response dial sessions. Provide the group with two arguments and they will instinctively prefer the one that helps them validate an existing perspective. Even when presented with the same fact, two people will come to startlingly different conclusions by running that fact through their own internal filters and imprinting it with their own perspective. The same is true inside companies where well-meaning corporate executives can't help putting a positive spin on the world and on new facts as they emerge.

Contrary to what some might like for us to believe, this filtering, this fact-finding mission to help support your point of view, is completely natural. There's nothing pernicious about looking for information to help bolster what you believe because humans have a natural inclination toward wanting to be right. Why would anyone want to be wrong? Somewhat ironically, most of us fancy ourselves smarter than those around us, so of course we're going to seek out facts, statistics, and arguments that we can use to sound smart and be right when the opportunity to do so arises.

The flip side of this inclination is that, on the whole, we're not really open-minded. In fact, we have become a nation that hears but rarely ever listens. We're a society that loves to debate for the sport of it rather than to achieve any real meeting of the minds. Our political conversations are littered with examples of people speaking past each other rather than with each other, often in the shrillest tones possible. Each side has cogent and detailed arguments to make its case, but the ensuing communication is a series of monologues rather than anything that can be called a dialogue. These communicators build a set of arguments that is persuasive to their current constituency but does nothing to engage those who are not yet already on board. The result is a lot of talking but little persuasion and almost no engagement.

Just turn on Sean Hannity or Keith Olbermann, who I mentioned earlier, or any of the thousands of partisan TV, radio, print, or Internet personalities. And ask yourself . . . have you ever changed your opinion as a result of one of their diatribes? Have you ever really given deep thought and reflection to a previously held belief or position based on one of their sixty-second riffs?

I didn't think so.

The result of this confirmation bias is an ever-widening gap between the opinions of those who agree with you and those who disagree. Ideologically, we are a nation populated by more self-described moderates (41 percent) than either conservatives (36 percent) or liberals (19 percent),[17] but on any given issue, the gap in agreement between those who are for and those who are against has become a chasm.

In the PTE, we do not have the luxury of preaching to the choir. We face skeptics at each step in our communication process and must change minds, attitudes, and behaviors along the way. Because we are presumed guilty until proven innocent, we must find a way to get into a conversation before we can ever hope to change minds. And without changing minds, attitudes ossify, and behaviors become rusted in place.

In romance, the term "engagement" refers to a period of getting to know another person before marriage. In business, it has a very similar meaning: trust revolves around relationships. In many cultures it is considered impolite to discuss business with someone before a long process of getting acquainted. And in the PTE, this is becoming everyone's culture.

More than ever before, we must *engage* our listeners as people before we can move forward with the heavy lifting of discussing an issue. This is true at a micro level in our dialogues with customers and prospects, and equally true at a macro level in our marketing and advertising.

The Rules of Engagement

So how do you build engagement phrases especially with someone you've never met before, like a prospective customer? We can break this process into what we call three "rules of engagement." While every rule may not show up in every dialogue, taken together they form the basis for language that engages.

Rule 1: Understand Their Truth

Sometimes when faced with the task of convincing someone of something—that taxes should be raised, that banks should be bailed out, or that your widget really is the best—we find it hard to comprehend why everyone doesn't share our point of view. At least I know I do. When I'm really passionate about an issue and I've read all there is to read, I often find myself perplexed that anyone can still think X or believe Y. Sometimes I just want to put my hands on the other person's shoulders and shake the crazy out of them! But that instinct, as natural as it may be, is the kiss of death to any communicator or salesperson, which is why you must learn not only how to control it, but also how to overcome it completely.

Earlier in the book I talked briefly about the concept of Your Truth and Their Truth—the idea that two people can have the exact same facts and access to information yet have entirely different views on a given topic. One of the most fundamental rules of engaging your audience is to understand Their Truth before saying a single word.

Understanding Their Truth is a two-step process. The first step is to do something that many advertising creatives do as part of their creative development: make sure you have a clear picture of your audience. To do this, I create "personas" that are detailed proxies for my target audience. Of course, there is no one customer for a product or idea, but by creating just a few (up to three) personas, you will be able to better understand, identify with, and communicate with your target audience. In building these personas, we give them an in-depth profile. Name, age, family situation, work situation, attitudes, likes, dislikes, etc. We even find a picture of someone who represents our target so that we can visualize this person as we prepare our messages.

The next step is to think in depth about the issue from their perspective. For this step, industry knowledge is extremely helpful. It is often quite easy for my clients to put themselves in the shoes of their critics or prospects, though it is something they rarely do. So we drill down into the issue or product and we build out what we believe to be Their Truth. When we have the opportunity to do research, we can confirm our hypotheses. But even without research, you can often make a reasonable guess.

These steps are so important because without knowing the other side's worldview, how they approach an issue, and what they already believe, you cannot possibly begin to have a meaningful conversation that's actually going to get you anywhere. What happens when you start a discussion without acknowledging Their Truth is that trust immediately begins to erode. Your skeptic hears what you're saying, but assumes you are ignoring her very valid concerns because you haven't taken the time to tease out and acknowledge the facets of Her Truth.

Let's go back to the biofuels example from the previous chapter. As part of that project, we conducted Instant Response dial groups in several European cities to learn what those outside the United States—a markedly more skeptical group when it comes to the environment—had to say about the idea of using corn and other organic materials as sources of energy.

What we learned is that one of the biggest pitfalls of communicating about biofuels is appearing *not* to respect your audience's already-held ideas and beliefs. It's one thing to speak to an audience that's relatively unaware of a subject—you have much more license to "teach them" and make sweeping assumptions. But when you talk to savvy Europeans, for example, about biofuels, assuming *anything* can get you in trouble quickly.

In this case, we knew (and confirmed in our research) that our audience was wary of biofuels' claims to be better for the environment. They don't believe they are better than regular fuels, on balance, because biofuels require more energy to produce and have only slightly less pollution when you look at the entire process. They worry about biofuel crops competing with food crops, especially in regions of the world where food is already so hard to come by. They think oil companies are only investing in biofuels to make more money or to look like they care about the environment when they really don't. And they don't think big oil companies have anyone's best interests at heart but their own.

Whether these things are true doesn't matter. Let me repeat that—whether these things are true doesn't matter. This is how these people feel. This is Their Truth. Communicators often think that they can change these core worldviews with their communication. But you can't—at least not without a lot of money and even more of the audience's attention. And you usually don't have either. So rather than trying to win a battle you are destined to lose, there is another more effective approach.

Accept their worldview. Understand it. And then use your knowledge of how they feel to engage them in a discussion.

In this case, it was essential to acknowledge and address the audience's concerns up front before you ever try to make your case *for* biofuels. It is the only approach that gives them permission to listen to the rest of what you have to say. And when we did it, we found that many skeptics were willing to listen and even agree with us by the end of the session.

One important note here: None of these statements were uncomfortable for our client to say. In fact, the client agreed with all of them. But their inclination was *not* to start the conversation by addressing these concerns. So we took some of the messages they would have saved until the end of the conversation and moved them right up front.

Words That Address Their Truth

✓ Biofuels will not compete with the world's food supply.
✓ Biofuels are renewable and sustainable.
✓ Our practices will be respectful of both people and our planet.
✓ The solutions will be affordable and accessible.

Rule 2: Find Common Ground

If you only take away one thing from this section of the book, please remember this: You *must* get people to listen to what you're saying before you can have a dialogue. Otherwise, you'll have two monologues.

Over and over again, we see that good messages fail because they get ahead of the listener. They attempt to persuade before they engage by jumping right into the meat of the argument without setting up the proper foundation upon which to build the conversation. And in doing so, the listener ceases to listen, rendering all arguments moot. Eventually you're left sitting there with a cold cup of coffee talking to yourself.

The language of trust is built on a foundation of engagement. In order to communicate effectively, you must build messages that start by getting the listeners to nod their heads in agreement, which lets you know they're actually listening. You must seek messages that create common ground or consensus first, and only then do you move on to messages that seek to persuade, sell, or change attitudes. This process of engagement is extremely important to building trust and starting a fruitful conversation, yet it is often forgotten or willfully ignored.

Just raise the issue of "tort reform" or, as we call it, "lawsuit abuse reform," and you will see most politically engaged Americans quickly take sides. Opponents of tort reform will quickly deliver a litany of arguments around the idea that people who are wronged must always get their day in court, that the justice system is stacked against the little guy, and that companies that do wrong should be penalized and made an example of.

Supporters of lawsuit abuse reform will talk about a "lawsuit lottery" that is dominated by frivolous lawsuits driving up the cost of insurance and health care, creating a culture of blame throughout our society. Trying to have a civil discussion on a topic like this is about as likely as a friendly barbeque with Bill O'Reilly and Keith Olbermann.

The reality is that some people are so entrenched and engaged on this issue that they will never change their minds. They feel like they've heard all the arguments, know all the facts, and refuse to entertain any more conversation on a topic that, in their minds, is clearly settled. But for many, there is an opportunity to change minds. The challenge is finding a way in—to get the opposition to listen.

If you support lawsuit abuse reform but start the conversation by attacking the trial lawyers and arguing that the people who sue are just out to get rich, the conversation ends. If you reject the other side's worldview from the outset, you cannot begin a conversation. Instead, the answer is to find areas of common ground as a foundation for the discussion. You need to start with the areas in which we can all agree, and proceed from there.

For example, we can start with specific problems in the health care or legal system. We can talk about the importance of having hospitals and doctors close to population centers. We can talk about people being treated fairly. We can talk about the desire to wring excessive costs out of the legal system. We can find the places where we both agree on larger issues as a starting point for a real exchange of ideas, opinions, and arguments. Having engaged the other side's interest in the issue, we can then have a real debate about the need for reform and have a real chance of changing minds.

Putting these broad, noncontroversial statements and general principles up front allows you to start the discussion on neutral ground. If the tone at the beginning of the conversation is one where you're already agreeing, it makes it much easier for your audience to follow you as you move along. Conversely, when you start out in a combative way, by saying, "You're wrong" or "I just don't think you're right about this issue," you immediately put the listener on the defensive. They feel a need to defend themselves, to be right, to fight back, which in almost every case will completely destroy your ability to convince them of anything. Why should someone be open to a meaningful discussion when you've already claimed they're wrong and we need to fix their broken point of view?

Here's something to think about: Watch two people talk some time, and you will notice something interesting. People almost never, ever, acknowledge each other.

Once in a while, I appear on the Fox News program *Strategy Room* to discuss various issues, usually surrounded by a group of people I consider to be friends and colleagues. These people are about as smart as they come, but if you listen closely, they clamor for attention like my spirited Eastern European ancestors talking over each other at the dinner table. Even when they agree with each other, most of them jump in quickly to let their own views be heard.

This is how most of us communicate most of the time. It's acceptable in this case because these commentators are really just there to entertain (I could write a whole other book about how disheartening it is that news has become entertainment, but I'll try to stay focused for now). But when I'm off the air and meeting with a client, I have to do a lot of listening, acknowledging, and validating—not just to respect my client, but because it sends out one of the most powerful signs possible: I'm listening and I care about what you're saying, so you can trust me.

Rule 3: Ask and You Shall Receive

The goal of engagement is to get people talking—and ideally, to put them at the center of the dialogue. Asking questions is often the quickest way there.

We often ask a question ourselves when we give speeches: "How many of you have gone to dinner with people who talk constantly about themselves?" Without fail, people raise their hands high with frustrated acknowledgment. The same is true in sales situations. Rather than discovering what a customer or voter really wants, too many selling conversations are completely one-sided. Conversely, when people sit down with someone who asks them meaningful, sincere questions, it often creates a very close and collegial relationship. Once upon a time, the rule was "The more you tell, the more you sell." Not anymore. In Bill Maher style, the new rule is "The more you ask, the more you engage." But you have to ask the right questions: you can't just take your agenda and stick a question mark at the end of it. Here are some examples of really bad questions:

- Leading questions: Think about parents who ask their children, "Do you think it's time to clean up your room?" They have no real interest in what these children think; they are just pushing their agenda.

- Throwaway questions: When people ask you, "How are you doing?" are they really expecting a detailed answer? Statements like these are a figure of speech, not an actual question.

- Hypothetical questions: When a financial advisor asks you, "What if I could offer you 7 percent on a AAA-rated bond?" they usually have no interest in any answer other than, "I'd purchase it."

On top of these, the history of sales is littered with a particularly insidious type of bad question: the ones that circle around the self-interest of the salesperson. Here are some examples that we all commonly hear:

"Are you ready to buy a car today?"
"How much are you prepared to invest?"
"Can I interest you in the extended warranty?"
"Would you like fries with that?"

You could call these "Lady Godiva" questions, because they have a naked agenda that is visible to everyone. Psychologists call this "motivational interviewing." Sales professionals call it "qualifying and upselling." Consumers call it annoying. And whatever you call it, it takes you far from a place of trust between you and the consumer.

Engagement questions focus in the other direction, toward the interests of the other person. They are closer to what you might ask someone on a date versus an interview—not in the sense of flirting, but in getting people to share more about themselves.

So what do these good questions look like?

First, the best questions are ones you don't know the answer to. Good questions are designed to learn what the other person *wants*, as opposed to what the other person will *buy*. Compare these questions and see what we mean:

Asking About Sales	Asking About Wants
Are you concerned about security for your family?	What are your biggest concerns?
Would you like to see how little it costs to upgrade to premium service?	What kinds of services are important to you?
If I made you this offer today, would you be interested?	What would an ideal package look like for you?

Second, good questions let the other person set the agenda, so you can react to it. Customers usually know what you are there for and what you can do for them: they aren't going to ask an automotive salesperson to give them financial advice, or vice versa. So you are safer than you think handing the agenda to the client with open, general questions.

This part feels a little scary to traditional salespeople. We were trained to use questions to focus customers and close in for the kill: for example, the classic "choice" close where you ask someone, "Would you like this in red or in blue?" But today's consumer is much more likely to respond with a hasty, "Neither of these, thanks, I am still thinking about this." Nowadays you would fare much better by asking them where they would like the process to go, or how you can be of assistance.

Finally, good questions are open ones, as opposed to closed questions with a yes or no answer. Closed questions put you in control, while open ones hand the floor to the customer. For example, instead of asking, "Is this feature important?" start thinking in terms of "What features matter to you?" Open questions lead to answers, and curiosity leads to connections.

It is tough for traditional salespeople to ask questions like these because they go against some things they were taught: control the conversation, frame the offer, and close the deal. Here you are handing the reins to the customers, and they might steer the conversation in a direction you didn't intend.

But that's exactly what you want going forward. When you hear your customer's wants and needs, unplugged, you are being given opportunities to build trust by both asking and responding. This, in turn, creates the kind of long-term relationships that will carry you far beyond today's sale. So take the leap of faith and put this dialogue in the hands of your customers, and let them start building a productive relationship for you.

Michael Dukakis:
The High Cost of Low Engagement

The second debate of the 1988 campaign for president of the United States, between challengers George H. W. Bush and Michael Dukakis, kicked off with a simple question from veteran CNN anchor Bernard Shaw: "Governor (Dukakis), if Kitty Dukakis were raped and murdered, would you favor an irrevocable death penalty for the killer?"

Dukakis responded with something that may have hastened the death of his campaign—a long-winded technical answer that focused on his support of legislation for the war on drugs. Without so much as a nod to how he would feel about his wife being a crime victim, he quickly noted his opposition to capital punishment, and then went on at length about things like better education and the need for a hemispheric summit.

When it was Vice President Bush's turn to respond, he wasted no time sharing genuine emotions: "Some crimes are so heinous, so brutal, so outrageous ... I do believe in the death penalty, and I think it is a deterrent, and I believe we need it ... we just have an honest difference of opinion: I support it and he doesn't."

For many people, this exchange cemented a growing reputation for Dukakis of being aloof and distant. A *Saturday Night Live* television skit soon portrayed him as a cold, emotionless alien under the control of a colony from outer space, while others contrasted his lack of passion with his Greek heritage by calling him "Zorba the Clerk." After the debate, Dukakis—who once enjoyed a fifteen-point lead over Bush—never recovered in the polls and went on to lose the 1988 contest by an electoral landslide.[18]

A Case Study of Engagement

The Pharmaceutical Industry

The pharmaceutical industry is one example of a business that learned the hard way to stop talking about drugs and start talking about people.

Emotional distrust with corporate America has really sunk its teeth into the pharmaceutical industry. Americans don't like anything *big*, and big pharma has come to represent corporate America at its biggest and baddest.

Back in 2006, I conducted extensive research across the United States about the pharmaceutical industry. Even then—in the midst of an economic boom—I found a level of consumer anger that went well beyond high drug costs and safety issues. In short, Americans felt the pharmaceutical industry put itself, its CEOs, and its shareholders ahead of its customers. They saw a lack of accountability, a lack of transparency, and a lack of business ethics around every corner and dripping out of every annual report. And they responded by ranking the industry as one of those most in need of government oversight, more so than even defense contractors and the private equity industry.

It didn't matter that most Americans personally benefit, or know people who personally benefit, from its innovative medications. They considered these medications to be necessary evils, from an industry that was taking money away from them even as they prolonged and improved their lives. In essence, they felt like hostages, and as consumers they resented feeling like they had no control. This was Their Truth.

When we talked to these people, we found a deep-seated and widely held worldview that, more than anything else, was driving the negative perceptions of the industry:

1. **Big pharma is addicted to treatment.** People felt that the pharmaceutical industry was not interested in curing or preventing disease—only in treating conditions, both perceived and real, with long-term prescriptions. Some even felt the industry had cures for cancer that it kept hidden in the closets of its labs!

2. **Greed drives the cost of prescriptions.** Most Americans believe that the industry spends more money on advertising than it does on R&D. An even larger majority believed that advertising, excessive profits, and CEO pay were the three factors most responsible for the high prices of prescription drugs.

3. **Profits ahead of patients.** People blamed the pharmaceutical industry for charging lower prices outside the country than in the United States, and for the fact that the Medicare system can't negotiate prices. And they overwhelmingly believed that profits came first in an industry that should be devoted to people.

And then there was the question of advertising. Americans accept advertising for cell phones and cars, but not for their medications. Similarly, they accept high prices for luxury items but not lifesaving drugs. The reason is simple: though patients can choose not to take a medication they need, they do not consider this a "choice."

As a result, it seemed hard to engage the American people in a rational discussion about the pharmaceutical industry, because they approached the subject from a completely different perspective. They were not wrong. They were not irrational. Their perspective was simply different from the industry's. Their Truth didn't align with the pharmaceutical industry's Truth.

To address these issues, we conducted Instant Response dial sessions in seven cities and tested over three hours of messages, some of which were based on the public interviews by pharmaceutical industry CEOs and some of which were brand new. We also conducted a nationwide survey among one thousand registered voters, including an oversample of Americans fifty-five and older to make sure the results really reflected the part of the public most impacted by prescription drugs—America's seniors. Our goal was to see what messages would both reflect the reality of this industry and engage the public, in a way that could create a more authentic dialogue moving forward.

Looking at the three core areas of concern mentioned previously, we first looked at the idea that pharmaceutical manufacturers were purely focused on "treatment." The industry needed to better articulate its view that drugs were part of a continuum that started with prevention and a healthy lifestyle. Here is one such message that worked in our testing:

> As a society, far too often we look to pills to solve our problems. Taking medication should never be the first step in living a healthy, productive life. A healthy diet, exercise, and routine examinations should *always* be step number one.
>
> As individuals, we should work to know what routine is best for us: what foods we should avoid, and what exercises may actually harm us. We should empower ourselves to live healthier so we don't need medications—or even worse, hospital visits or surgery.

But when it becomes clear we still have a medical problem, *that's* where pharmaceuticals should come in. Our responsibility as an industry is first to help you live healthier lives, and to be there if and when you still need us.

Coming back to our rules of engagement, we started by accepting Their Truth—that too many people take too many pills. Then we found something to agree on—that people should do what they can to stay healthy so they can avoid needing pills. And then we talked about the appropriate place for medications—when preventive care has failed to resolve a medical problem.

Next was the belief that "greed" drives the industry. Even though pharmaceutical company profit margins actually are under 15 percent—a figure people felt was acceptable in our testing—and much of these profits are reinvested in research and new product development, people were wary of the financial motivations of big pharma.

There is a simple reason for much of this distrust. People struggle with the cost of their medications—particularly in lower income brackets, and people between forty and sixty-five who often needed medication but were not old enough to qualify for government prescription drug assistance. By more than two to one, Americans believe that it is more important for the pharmaceutical industry to provide low or no-cost medications to low-income Americans than it is to increase the number of breakthrough medications.

From a communication perspective, we could either try to change their opinions about pharma profits and greed or we could give them more information about something they cared about—access to affordable medications. Because it is virtually impossible to change the perception that pharma profits are too high, we found that the best way to start changing minds about the pharma industry was to educate them more about the programs for low-income Americans that were already in place.

In fact, the pharmaceutical industry has extensive programs to help increase access to medications. People might think that more money should be spent or that the industry should lower prices across the board, but nearly everyone agreed that the more they learned about the industry's programs, the more their opinions of the industry improved. And we learned that the way to engage the public on the issue of "greed" was to talk about something else entirely.

Finally, there was the politically sensitive issue of drug prices in America versus the rest of the world. Most Americans knew that medications were more expensive in the United States than abroad, but few knew why. So engagement in this case was focused first on explicitly agreeing with and validating their perspective. The next step was to educate people about the real reasons for these disparities: a system where foreign governments can mandate prices, competing against an American system that is open, transparent, and fosters much more innovation. Here is a sample:

When you compare the prices patients pay for medications in other countries with the prices patients pay here in America, it is clear something is wrong. How can it be fair that Americans pay more than the rest of the world? The truth is that it's not fair. It's not right.

It is only fair that patients who suffer from the same conditions in different countries should pay the same price for that medication. Today, it is not the case. American patients tend to pay more for brand-name medications, and this isn't fair.

International law allows that gap in prices to happen. International law says that Canada, which has a government price control system, can tell us that we have to sell our medicine over there for 30 or 40 percent cheaper. If we don't like it, they can take our patents. They can steal our invention and simply manufacture it in their own company, and sell it to the rest of the world.

It's like being in the guillotine. You either play by their rules, or they chop your head off and take your invention.

Here again, we used the rules of engagement. We did not challenge their worldview up front. Instead, we agreed with them and found common ground. We then could have a discussion about the reasons behind the issue in an environment where they were, at least, willing to consider the industry's perspective.

In this example we had the benefit of research to test a wide range of articulations and find the best words, phrases, and messages to use. But putting this process into practice can be done easily with—or without—research. The key is to understand the steps and to recognize the need to engage before you discuss. Let's take another example and assume I am trying to get an investor to invest in a new business idea I have. This investor sees plenty of entrepreneurs and has heard every kind of pitch out there. My business is another new social media site in a universe where more and more are popping up every day. I would have a plan for each of these steps before walking into the meeting.

Step 1: Who is my audience? My investor knows a lot about social media. He has also been burned by investments that promised big payouts that never materialized. He is much more skeptical of new business models and of unproven management.

Step 2: What is Their Truth? New platforms are hard to build and very few make it. The best idea isn't necessarily enough to be successful—companies need to be able to manage their business and generate buzz better than the competition. Companies that claim to have a wide range of revenue opportunities often don't have any that will be successful.

Step 3: How do I engage? Here I might come up with a list of questions designed to confirm that my assumptions about the investor are true. These questions are designed to engage the investor and also to help me to personalize my response. Questions might be: So what do you think are the biggest challenges new companies face in becoming successful? Or what are the metrics that you find most important in evaluating companies?

As an alternative, I might simply take what I already believe to be His Truth and start to address his concerns. I would reorder my presentation to emphasize in concrete terms the steps I am taking to generate revenues and get to profitability. Before talking about the huge potential of this idea, I would talk about the importance of creating a sustainable business. Instead of using Twitter and Facebook as an example—as if I could be as successful as either—I would talk about my management team and the successes each member has had. Instead of cool graphics, I would focus on clearly presenting data. And instead of telling him about every single revenue opportunity that might exist, I would focus on the ones that will make or break the business.

I would never challenge his worldview. Instead, I would tailor my approach to it. And if I did it well, I would never have to ask for money. He would offer it himself.

From Aspirin to People

Perhaps one of the best examples of putting engagement before dialogue is the recent advertising for over-the-counter medicines. Take Bayer aspirin, for example.

In the 1960s, Bayer's advertising was all about the product. In one ad, a stern-looking announcer starts right in with, "What's the best way to reduce the fever of a cold or virus infection? Bayer aspirin." Pointing to a large sign reading, "Doctors recommend aspirin," he then states how this drug is repeatedly recommended in public health articles, medical journals, and personal consultations.

Next, as he drops aspirin into a long, spiral tube attached to a laboratory flask, he talks about Bayer's instant flaking action, a shower of tiny flakes so gentle and so quickly absorbed that Bayer is ready to go to work instantly. Finally, to make sure you don't forget, he walks over and points to the sign to remind you again that "doctors recommend aspirin to reduce fever and make you feel better fast." All told, within thirty seconds he had spoken or pointed to the word "aspirin" at least half a dozen times.

Twenty years later in the 1980s, not much had changed. One ad opens with a glowing full-screen Bayer aspirin tablet, as another deep voice gravely intones, "It's here—the better-tolerated aspirin—new, improved Bayer aspirin, with the patented micro-thin coating," before demonstrating its less chalky properties on one of two identical silhouette heads. All told, the words "Bayer" and "aspirin" are stated five times apiece within the spot's thirty seconds.

Today, it's all about the people, not the medicine. One recent ad shows home improvement celebrity Ty Pennington relaxing at a kitchen table with a Bayer aspirin user as he says, "So Joe here keeps his company's books straight—and runs a pretty tight ship at home." Joe replies that as a fifteen-year cancer survivor, health is very important to him. Only after nearly half the ad is over does the brand name even get mentioned—briefly—as Joe describes how his doctor tells him to take it for his heart.

For most of this ad, the spokesperson Ty is actually just listening, making good eye contact and nodding attentively as Joe speaks—and it isn't until twenty seconds into the ad that you even hear the word "aspirin." But most people would agree that this spot is much more effective than those from decades ago.

Moving from Monologue to Dialogue

Engaging your audience is more than just a good communication skill. It has become the foundation of twenty-first-century marketing, with terms like "brand engagement" and "consumer engagement" becoming part of the lingo of the profession. And beyond the trendy buzz phrases, nearly anyone working in mass-market advertising realizes that the future lies in creating a conversation with consumers, not just broadcasting messages to them.

Our challenge from here is to take this concept from Madison Avenue to Main Street, and start changing the way we all communicate. Most salespeople still live in an age of features, jargon, and "closing phrases," in a world that has moved past all of these more quickly than anyone realized. In an era of mistrust, we need to get people talking about their favorite subjects—themselves—and to realize that we may only have one opportunity to do so.

The supreme irony is that we now live in a world where everything can be measured, including the impact of the words we say, and these high-tech measurements are pointing us toward a world that our great-grandparents understood long ago in their small businesses and country stores: one where you build a relationship with people first, long before you get down to the business of buying and selling. It starts with engaging people and then progresses from there to authentic and productive dialogue.

When humorist Will Rogers noted that "A stranger is just a friend I haven't met yet" nearly a century ago, he was in a very real sense capturing part of today's mind-set for creating trust. When you engage people as friends you haven't met yet, you start building the personal relationships that will guide you past today's walls of initial skepticism. This, in turn, can become the basis for a level of success that now eludes so many who cannot see beyond their own product brochures.

8

It's Not About You: Putting Their Interests Before Yours

It's bigger than you and me . . . It's all about me.

—Stephen Colbert

The Japanese martial art of aikido stands in complete opposition to how most people view combat. It teaches followers to flow with the rhythm of their opponents instead of resisting them. By harnessing the opponent's energy, the fighter gains maximum power and leverage to bring a physical conflict to an end. What makes aikido different from other martial arts is that it was designed to allow practitioners to defend themselves while also protecting their attacker from injury. Probably for this reason, it has been translated by some as the "way of harmonious spirit."[19] Now compare this to the many people who seek to sell ideas or overcome objections. No aikido here. Instead, these conversations are more like a typical movie scene of hand-to-hand combat. Two fighters face off against one another. Each uses every ounce of strength because these battles are a zero-sum game in which there is one winner and one loser. Each defends their own interests. As one pushes, the other pushes back. All we're missing is "POW" and "KA-BAM" action bubbles, and our fight sequence will be complete. Rather than seeking a middle ground, these conversations often seem like a battle to the death, where it is more important to prove a point than it is to achieve a goal.

The last chapter was about getting skeptics to listen to what you have to say even when they are inclined to disagree with or ignore you. To continue (and hopefully not torture) the fighting metaphor, engagement is about getting your audience in the ring. Now you can move into the sales conversation. Your audience is still skeptical, but they are at least willing to listen.

In sales, the process may be more subtle than hand-to-hand combat, but often the result is the same. Salespeople see the process of selling as one of convincing their prospect of the merits of the product while batting away objections in the strongest possible terms. The philosophy is that objections must be overcome—or defeated—in order to win the sale. Any room for doubt creates risk that the prospect will walk away, so many salespeople learn to think about the objections ahead of time so they can respond with a forceful and convincing argument.

In the last chapter, I talked about how you must understand your audience's truth so that you can present messages that anticipate their objections at the beginning of your sales pitch. At this point, your audience will continue to have questions and objections as they gather more information, but they are of a more specific nature. In sales, they may be about price (where before it was about whether they would even consider the product at any price). For issue communications, engagement objections tend to relate to philosophy while objections at this point relate to specific policy prescriptions. In other words, to engage the audience you need to address their higher-order concerns. In the discussion phase we are now into the specifics.

What works at this stage is much more like aikido than like a traditional sales pitch. Rather than pushing your idea or your product, the most effective approach to build trust and achieve your goal is to let the audience lead. Put their interests first. Acknowledge their concerns first. Accept their point of view first. And in the process become their advocate even at those precise moments where they might disagree with you or seem to be putting your sale at risk.

Take the case where someone test-drives a car at your dealership. She emerges from the driver's seat, walks back to your desk, and states that she likes the car a lot, but that it has a lot of wind noise. How do you respond? Most people will defend the sale like a mother bear protects her cubs, saying things like:

- "There are so many other benefits to this car, like the ride, the gas mileage, and the value."

- "You'll get used to that in time. It just sounds a little different than what you're used to."

- "If you get the premium stereo option, you won't even notice the wind."

Each of these statements serves a very powerful purpose with today's consumer: they destroy your credibility. So now let's try another approach:

"Is noise an important factor for you? I tend to pay attention to things like this, because even small issues can loom larger after you've owned a car for a while. If you'd like, I can show you the technical data we have on the interior noise level in this car, so we can compare it with others."

This second approach works better than the first nearly every time. Why? Because just as the first salesperson is pushing his point of view, the prospect is likely to push back with hers.

Meanwhile the second salesperson has positioned himself as her ally. Rather than pushing his own point of view, the second salesperson is acting as an arbiter of information while putting the prospect in control.

This is a common finding in our research. Consumers come to the table with built-in concerns about products they are considering or issues they are evaluating. These concerns may seem subtle, but they are most often the tip of the philosophical iceberg. In other words, they represent something much larger. The car shopper may have dealt with noise for years with her last car or she may be an audiophile who really cares about a quiet driving experience. For her, telling her she will get used to it or changing the subject will not change her mind. In fact, it will probably backfire completely.

Instead, there is only one path to building credibility and getting to the sale: Help her better understand the noise issue as well as all the other benefits of the car. Then put her in a position to make up her own mind. Because, as .38 Special so accurately sang, "If you cling too tightly, you're gonna lose control."

Lead with the Other Person

Think about those conversations you've had with people who only talk about themselves. If you had a handheld dial, you would probably turn it down and down and down as you listened to them go on and on without ever engaging you in a dialogue. Sadly, what seems so obviously inappropriate in a personal situation is standard practice when it comes to selling issues and products. When given the opportunity to sell, most communicators do. And they resort to their set of product features or standard talking points without taking the time to think about to whom they are selling or why the buyer would want to buy. In part, this may be because it is easier to learn about the features of a product or the arguments to support an issue than it is to tailor either of them to the specific needs of the listener. More often it is simply the result of the fact that we are raised to believe that the art of "persuasion" is about making the most convincing arguments in an effort to "win someone over" to your side. In other words, to beat them into submission.

What is interesting is that the best salespeople today are nearly always the ones who put their customers' interests before their own. Listen to a panel of high–net worth individuals, for example, sharing the best thing about their current financial advisor:

- "Very attentive and very responsive to my statements—he pays attention, he moves forward—I love that, he's just right there with me."

- "Accessible—he gets back to you promptly."

- "Understands my goals and asks about them frequently."

- "Knows my risk situation and what my comfort level is."

- "He's made me money."

- "He's patient in answering any questions I may have—he listens and then he answers."

All but one of these people are talking about how well the advisor interacts with them, and only one is talking about the product he sells: financial performance. In the health care arena, the doctors that are perceived as the highest quality and least likely to be sued for malpractice are not the ones like House who are the best diagnosticians; they are the doctors who take the extra few moments with the patient to look them in the eye and answer their questions. And on issue after issue, we find that the most "persuasive" arguments are the ones that are the least focused on convincing the listener to accept a position.

Notice a trend here? In each case, the most effective approach is the one that puts the audience's interest before the communicator's. It places a premium on building trust and puts selling at the end of the conversation. In this chapter I lay out a three-step approach for creating high-plausibility responses, particularly when the listener is skeptical, that ties in with our research:

- Acknowledge and validate the other person.

- Agree in first person—and if possible, amplify the other person's concerns.

- Add new, unbiased information.

Each of these steps creates a new kind of influence: one whose purpose is not to persuade the other person toward your point of view, but rather to put factors on the table that both parties can sort, weigh, balance, and consider to come to a decision.

Don't Buy Our Product

In the last few years, there has been an interesting trend in some industries: advertisements and websites designed to encourage people to use less of their product. For example:

- Energy giant Chevron has advertisements on the public transit system of major cities, with messages such as "I will unplug things more" or "I will at last consider a hybrid" designed to encourage people to use less energy—and targeted at people who are already motivated to give up their cars and use mass transportation.

- Anheuser-Busch's Beeresponsible campaign targets key issues in alcohol abuse, such as underage consumption, campus binge drinking, and drunk driving. An example of one of its position statements: "At Anheuser-Busch we don't want anyone consuming our products illegally—ever. After all, we're parents too—sharing the same concerns as every other parent about these issues."

- And then there is the Tylenol example and the underlying Stop. Think. Tylenol. campaign discussed in chapter 1.

None of these companies are trying to put themselves out of business. But each of these companies has recognized that they faced significant negative issues associated with their businesses. They could have chosen to fight the underlying argument—to reject the need for conservation, responsible drinking, or care when taking medications. Instead, each chose to address it head-on by acknowledging the issue and trying to help the consumer avoid the problem. Some people will still say that this is a crass effort to avoid litigation or regulation, but chances are that many more looked at these campaigns and saw companies making an effort to do something for their customers other than selling a product. And with that they likely gained a little bit of trust.[20]

Step 1: Acknowledge and Validate the Other Person

Let's assume that we have already engaged our audience in a conversation. We have achieved our first milestone: they are willing to listen to what we have to say. We understand where they are coming from (Their Truth). We have found some common ground. Or maybe we have asked them a few questions to better understand their perspective about the product or issue. We have not yet tried to convince them to buy what we are selling. And yet we know that they have concerns. Now what?

Rather than using this opportunity with your captive audience to start with the most compelling benefits and features of your product, we want you to start with your own area of greatest vulnerability. Rather than completing your pitch and then waiting to overcome objections, we want you to anticipate them. Acknowledge them. Validate them. Because until you do, the skeptic never really starts to listen.

First, let's be clear about what we mean by these terms. (Let me also caveat this by acknowledging up front that dissecting this process will likely feel a bit uncomfortable because the first steps, on their own, do not themselves build trust. It is the full process outlined later.) "Acknowledge" and "validate" have different meanings that complement each other. To acknowledge someone means to accept another person's view of the world as how he or she sees things, *whether or not you agree with this view*. Here is an example of a good acknowledgment:

> **Jayne:** I get uncomfortable with the idea of locking up my money in any one investment.

Advisor: It sounds like liquidity and access to your money is very important to you.

Here's another:

Harris: I refuse to support health care reform if it means that government bureaucrats will make decisions about my health.

Elected official: Health care is a very personal issue, and I recognize that you want to make sure that reform doesn't have a negative impact on the way you get health care today.

If you break down the mechanics of acknowledgment, it involves taking the other person's statements, paraphrasing them in your own words, and then verifying them with the other person. It combines the most soothing sound in the world—namely, the speaker's own thoughts and feelings—within a zone of acceptance and interest.

Acknowledgment feels natural when you agree with someone. What you probably don't realize is that it is also safe to do this, and in fact all the more important to do so, when you disagree. Simply put, acknowledgment creates connection.

Validation takes this process a step further, and makes it clear to the other person that their feelings are *valid*. Here is an example:

Max: You cannot proclaim to be an environmentally friendly company as long as your packaging is made from nonrecyclable materials.

Company: We recognize that, like many of our customers, you want to do business with companies that take responsibility for the products they sell and the waste they create.

You still may or may not agree with the other person, but you can almost always make it clear that others share their opinion, and that many consider it to be a legitimate view of the world. If you sell for a living, making statements like these can be difficult because you are validating—rather than overcoming—the objection. Customers are shying away from your products (and your commission), and here you are implying to them that it is okay to feel that way. In fact, it's incredibly counterintuitive, and sometimes—let's be realistic . . . oftentimes—it's difficult to do. But we are learning that rising above your interests to share someone else's worldview is not only the best way to connect with your clients, but the only way.

Acknowledgment and validation accomplish a number of goals on the path to building trust. They help you demonstrate:

1. That you are listening to what the other person is saying (itself no small feat).

2. That you understand their concern and can place it into a context that is larger than just them. In other words, that they are not alone in how they see things.

3. That they are still in control of the conversation.

Because mistrust is fueled by the feeling that you are biased and don't understand, your first goal is to put that perception to rest right away. Acknowledgment and validation are the most effective tools to help you do that.

Preemptive Acknowledgment

Many baby boomers remember actor James Garner as suave detective Jim Rockford from the television series *The Rockford Files*. Today, at age eighty, a much older and vulnerable-looking Garner now stars as a pitchman for Financial Freedom, a company marketing reverse mortgages to senior citizens.

His ad for Financial Freedom is powerful because instead of being a glib celebrity, he comes across as a fellow everyman in a rumpled sweater vest—another senior citizen trying to make the right decisions with his money. He builds trust by acknowledging the natural skepticism of his audience, looking into the camera, and stating, "I was reluctant to talk about reverse mortgages myself, because I didn't have the facts." Then he encourages viewers to learn more, not to simply buy.

Garner's message is effective because it uses a technique known as *preemptive acknowledgment* to address concerns and build trust. Older home owners are understandably cautious about handing over their house title to a financial company in return for a monthly income. So the focus of the ad is on learning, using a free educational video, and the closest Garner comes to a pitch is saying, "I think you should at least look into it."

Preemptive acknowledgment has been used for years to address concerns head-on. For example, in 1969, an advertisement for the Volkswagen Beetle showed a picture of the lunar landing module with the caption "It's ugly, but it gets you there." Likewise, a recent ad for the Toyota Prius claimed that it was not the prettiest car, and not the least expensive, but may be the best one for your family. Both are part of a growing trend where companies take the public's biggest objections, and put them front and center in their advertising.

Step 2: Agree in First Person—and If Possible, Amplify the Other Person's Concerns

Now we get to the part that requires a little more emotional investment: finding points of agreement and amplifying them.

This concept flies in the face of both human nature and traditional sales logic. We are programmed to "respond to objections," but
the language of trust involves something entirely different: not only
acknowledging and validating another person's concerns, but enhanc-
ing them with your own information. In other words, when someone
challenges you, you find a way to *agree even more* with the speaker.

This is a bit like the Biblical passage that states, "Whoever takes
away your coat, do not withhold your shirt from him either."[21] Here,
you build trust by walking a mile in the other person's shoes, and
then—if possible—making it a mile and a half. Agreeing and then
amplifying concerns is as powerful as it is counterintuitive.

Suppose you are an executive in the music industry. You are faced
with the growing epidemic of piracy that has spread across the globe
and far beyond its roots among teenagers. Now people in almost
every age group are seeking out copies of your songs online. From a
legal perspective, there is little question that downloading is a viola-
tion of copyright and therefore illegal. Yet efforts to sue downloaders
have created a public relations nightmare. In fact, our research has
shown that even members of the news media and legislative staffers
on Capitol Hill believe that the music industry itself is to blame for
piracy problems.

So how do you start to turn the tide and limit public acceptance
of illegal downloading? Start by agreeing with the other side's point
of view. Below are three research-tested recommendations we made
to the industry:

TURNING THE TIDE

- Talk about *your responsibility* for some of the downloading. A majority of journalists believed that people who left the doors of their houses unlocked were at least partially responsible if they were robbed during the night. They saw the industry as doing just that with music. They demanded that the industry do its part to protect its content from free and easy theft. *By talking about your responsibility for making sure that your property is protected, you weaken your audience's resistance to your position.* As one journalist said, "Copyrights should be protected by the people who want them protected."

- Talk about the need for *balance*. You need to stake yourself in the middle of the road and avoid the two extremes in the intellectual property debate: the extreme of discarding intellectual property protections completely in an orgy of free downloading and the opposite extreme of siccing the FBI on any thirteen-year-old who illegally downloads *Shrek* off of the Internet. You must articulate a *middle ground* in which everyone takes some of the responsibility for putting an end to illegal downloading.

- Talk about the need to *meet consumers halfway*. You need to remember that your audience is not just potential criminals, but also active consumers. So talk to them like consumers. Talk about how you've gone the extra mile to change your business model for them. Offer them the opportunity to at least meet you in the middle by using your new, legal products.

Consumers had clearly communicated their concerns. And the industry had to acknowledge and accept the validity of those concerns if it hoped to rebuild trust. In this case, it had to do away with the simplistic notion that all downloading is stealing and replace it with a more complex idea that both parties have a responsibility to take steps that would result in less piracy.

Now suppose that clients of yours have a substantial percentage of their assets in the stock market. There has been a downturn over the last month, and this couple has lost 20 percent of the value of their holdings on paper. They are now speaking with you—their financial advisor—before deciding what to do. First, let's look at the traditional approach of overcoming objections.

> **Susie:** I wonder if we should pull our money out of the market. We've lost over $70,000 since the first of the year.
>
> **Advisor:** Market corrections like these are exactly the time that people should be *buying* stocks. You want to buy low and sell high, and there are some terrific bargains out there. Don't let fear keep you from missing out on an opportunity that tracks the natural cycles of the market.

On paper, this approach appears to be speaking to the couple's interests, but it is poisoned by a tone of "me, me, me" advocacy that speaks to one option alone. Worse, it devalues the concerns that the couple brought to the table: it avoids the subject of their losses like an ugly stepchild. These words push an agenda that resonates with the advisor's financial interests at the expense of building trust and credibility.

Now let's lead by taking the couple's objections, acknowledging and validating them, and then amplifying these concerns:

Susie: I wonder if we should pull our money out of the market. We've lost over $70,000 since the first of the year.

Advisor: You have a good point, Susie. A typical bear market correction is 30 percent, but the current correction is 38 percent. That is lower than I have seen it in a long time. Let's look at your investment time horizon and discuss some options.

Now you have built instant credibility. You have embraced the other person's objection, amplified it with your own perspective, and then presented yourself as a source of knowledge. In the process you have made a strong case for people to learn from you, whether they are buying from you or not.

Amplifying concerns is particularly potent in a crisis. When a criminal tampered with Tylenol pain-relieving capsules in the early 1980s, Johnson & Johnson CEO James Burke went on national television to urge people to stop taking Tylenol and return their bottles to drugstores, telling people, "Don't risk it. Take the voucher so that when this crisis is over we can give you a product we both know is safe." The same was true in the case of JetBlue in the story recounted in chapter 2. Both of these companies went on to quickly regain their lost market share.[22]

So why don't most of us ever amplify the other person's concerns? Because we feel we are standing at the edge of a cliff, with two stark choices: agree and lose, or fight and win. But our testing has shown that exactly the opposite is usually true: we gain trust when we take full ownership of another person's concerns, and lose it every time we brush them aside. So go ahead and jump off the cliff; there is almost always a soft landing of trust and credibility waiting for you.

Step 3: Add New, Unbiased Information

Go to the website for the auto insurance firm Progressive and you will see a real-time ticker on the main page comparing their rates for actual shoppers. Sometimes Progressive's rates are lower, and sometimes they are higher. But for Progressive, a firm that began insuring high-risk drivers with premium service, a key to its sales process is a transparent flow of information.

For each of us, information is the new font of credibility. Not just information that benefits our interests—we call that "spin"—but all relevant information. When you give people the facts to make a good decision, they trust you and come back to you, again and again.

We are always sharing information, every time we open our mouths, but unbiased information has a style of its own. Here are some examples of what we mean:

- A client questions the future of the financial markets, and you give her online resources to help her look at the performance of past crises and make her own judgment.

- A customer wants to book a trip through your travel agency, and instead of just giving him brochures, you share public websites where people post their own very frank opinions about hotels and restaurants in specific cities, to help him make a better decision.

- A consumer of personal care products questions the safety of your products and instead of pointing her to your website where you have carefully chosen to present a one-sided view of the debate about product safety, you refer her to a website where she can see all the proven research on the issue.

Some businesses even make it their focus to serve as a neutral source of information. Amazon.com encourages customers to rate products, post messages, and create linked informational "wiki" pages about the things it sells, and in turn lets authors post videos and blogs about their own books. And in an online world where anyone can comparison shop and get something a few cents cheaper, this sense of community and honesty keeps pulling people back to buy through Amazon.com.

The act of adding new information is a way to build a relationship with your customers, moving toward their view of the world with something that helps them. Take this example, where a financial client is wondering what kind of investment he should roll over his 401(k) funds into:

Morgan: I am leaving my job with about $120,000 in retirement assets, and I am wondering where to invest this money. I see growth funds, income funds, and equity funds, and I am not sure what to think.

Advisor: You've picked a good time to examine these things, before you invest such a large amount of money. I would like to take a couple of minutes and explain the difference between some of these funds to you.

First of all, I want you to know that a "growth" fund is not named that way because it will always grow. This is a somewhat euphemistic name for a fund for people who are willing to take more risk, in return for an investment that has more potential to grow. Next is the income fund: these tend to be more conservative investments that involve income-producing securities, such as common stock and convertible bonds. Equity funds tend to invest in large, highly capitalized companies and carry a moderate risk relative to the overall market.

Morgan: The problem is that this all sounds good to me! I want my stocks to grow, I would like to get income from my securities, and I want to have equity in major companies—but I'm sure that all of these funds don't perform the same, so I am wondering what to do in the short term.

Advisor: These are great questions. It is important to remember that the way a fund has performed in the past does not guarantee how it will perform in the future, and that these types of funds all have the potential to lose value as well as gain value. It all depends on how the market values the securities that these funds invest in.

One thing we can do is to look at the records of how these funds have performed in similar economic conditions, and in some cases, we can even play "what if" games to see how an investment years ago would be doing today. If you would like, I can give you some resources like these to help your own decision-making process.

What you are seeing here is a neutral, factual discussion based on adding new information. The advisor is educating the client about how different funds are invested, and offers resources to Morgan to explore their performance further. But note that there is no attempt to "sell" a particular product, or even ask Morgan to invest any money at all. This advisor's goal is to create a bond of trust that, unto itself, may become the incentive Morgan needs to make an investment.

Examples like these are a microcosm of a new style of communication that goes against the way most of us think, but is totally aligned with what we want as consumers ourselves. It isn't new: Any college textbook on influence and persuasion will discuss principles like providing information and speaking against our interests. But only lately has it become a required ticket of entry for gaining new customers—and a clear strategic advantage over the masses who still stick to old-school selling techniques.

But Don't Ever Tell Them What to Do

People want direction and guidance. But, they *never* want to be told what to do. I saw this clearly in the midst of a project for a philanthropic organization. Our goal: to create what we called a "language of generosity." We sought to develop a set of messages that would reduce the inertia or reluctance to give time or money to good causes. We weren't focused on any one cause, just on giving in general. Yet even when dealing with as altruistic an endeavor as this, we found that there were clear limits to the language we could use to motivate people to act. If we wanted to engage people—especially college students—and give them a reason to do more, we had to be very careful not to push too hard. So when we failed to be the unbiased provider of information and started to be the aggressive advocate for our position, we were rejected. We found that everyone agrees they *could* do more, but few felt that they should *have* to. Tell them they have a responsibility to give, and we heard a negative, visceral, knee-jerk rejection. Over and over again, we heard the same thing: "I don't like when they tell me to do it because it's a good thing . . . I don't want to be told what to do."

Words That Don't Work

All over the world, people are suffering. Even within your community, people need shelter, food, or education. And people are looking to you to give back. You have the ability and the capability to make a difference. Don't fall into the trap of indifference. Be aware of the problems around you. And donate your time to help those in need. It is your responsibility to promote a healthy future. It is your responsibility to promote our future. Without people giving back, there will be no future to enjoy.

You have probably seen or heard words like these before—charities that push you to make a decision. Companies that try to press you to buy a product. Or politicians who hound you for fundraising dollars. The biggest problem with this statement is that it failed the neutrality test. Rather than presenting reasons to give and leaving control with the audience, it went too far. It took control away and, in the process, failed to convince anyone to give.

Next is another approach to which people had a much more favorable response. You can see that it puts the audience in control but provides them with ideas, tools, and encouragement to give.

Words That Work

You don't have to travel far to help. Look around you. You can probably find a nearby soup kitchen or a homeless shelter to volunteer your time. Or a local hospital or school in need of additional funds for supplies. Chances are it will be easy to find a way to make an impact right in your own neighborhood.

Opportunities for you to give your time or money to a worthy cause
are all around you. And it can be as easy as walking down the block and
simply asking how you can help.

Putting People First:
A Language and a Mind-Set

The "theirs before yours" approach is, more than anything, a mind-
set as well as a style of communication. It is a mind-set that leads
communicators to become honest, trustworthy sources of facts and
information for people, instead of people who are always pushing an
agenda. Whether you are selling stocks or running for president, an
enlightened interest in those around you is now the first thing people
look for before they let you into their hearts, minds, and decision-
making process.

This mind-set involves a way of thinking and speaking that goes
far beyond addressing concerns: it speaks proactively to the other
person's interest. Recently I gave a presentation for a financial company, with a panel of high–net worth investors onstage with dials in
hand. As they watched, a financial advisor spoke on a video screen:

Today, this business is much different than it used to be. In the old
days, we were stockbrokers, and we were paid to generate transac-
tions. Today, I'm a consultant, and I give advice and counsel to my
clients. My relationship is one of partnership, and it is one based
on trust. What that role allows me to do is be on the same side of
the table as you are. Education is my responsibility; I want you to

be totally informed on the decisions you make, because it helps us make better decisions all the time.

As he spoke, the dial readings went up over 80, showing that he was really connecting with the panel. And when I debriefed them, I heard comments like, "My ears perked up when I heard the word 'you'" and "I felt he would put his money in the same funds he would recommend for me." His credibility and his desirability as an advisor both linked very strongly with his stated role as an information source.

Traditional salespeople are often taught to adhere to a sense of false bravado (for example, "I am confident, and so you should be too"). By comparison, authentic communication shares honest concerns and data. It starts in your head and your heart, and then comes out through the words you choose to say; you need to pull all of this together to succeed in today's environment.

This principle often goes by the name of servant leadership. It isn't a new concept: you can see it in the scriptures of most major religions and the biographies of many great leaders. But in the PTE, it is more critical than ever. When you expose your own vulnerability, give the other person information, and focus on the interests of others, you create a zone of trust that fundamentally changes the relationship.

9

That's Not What I Meant: Context Before Specifics

In Washington, the clearer a statement is, the more certain it is to be followed by a "clarification" when people realize what was said. The clearly racist comments made by Judge Sonia Sotomayor on the Berkeley campus in 2001 have forced the spinmasters to resort to their last-ditch excuse, that it was "taken out of context."

—Thomas Sowell,
Townhall.com, June 2, 2009

How many times have you heard the phrase "it was taken out of context" in the past few days, weeks, or months? It may not be quite as ubiquitous as Verizon's "Can you hear me now?" but it's certainly as recognizable. In fact, if you're reading this book, there's a good chance you've issued a similar statement at some point or at least thought it to yourself when something you said was misconstrued, misunderstood, or simply missed the mark.

There are times, as alleged in the opening quote, where this idea of "being taken out of context" is purely a political defense mechanism. There are many more times where comments are misconstrued because there was no context to be "taken out of." The speaker listed a set of facts or arguments assuming that they would be interpreted as intended. No narrative was developed or context provided. And in the absence of that context, the listener is able to draw his or her own conclusions, which are usually not the same conclusions as the speaker intended.

Too many communicators fall down at this point. They make the fatal assumption that their audience will interpret words and messages—or even so-called facts—as they intend them to be interpreted. And in so many cases, they are surprised when the audience applies a different interpretation.

In the last two chapters we talked about what it takes to get your skeptical audience to listen to what you have to say, and how to position the conversation to ensure that listeners feel that you have their interests in mind. This chapter is about the last mile—making sure that the specifics of your sales pitch are interpreted the way you want them to be. That is what context is all about.

Think about communication like a TV screen. If you were to go up to one and put your nose against it, you wouldn't be able to see what you're watching. You'd see the individual pixels, their color, how quickly they flicker off and on, but each one by itself wouldn't carry any real meaning. Now take a step back, any better? Take a few more steps back, how's that? Suddenly what were a few pixels that had no impact on you became a vivid image of a woman rescuing a child from a burning house. The disparate, seemingly void bits of light and information were turned into a moving narrative because you took a step back and were able to appreciate them in a larger scope.

That is context.

Context is the information—the extra hundred thousand pixels, the taking a step back—that allows us to put things into perspective so they can make sense. Without context it's often very hard for us to make sense of and process the vast amounts of information that bombard us every single day.

Just imagine the health care debate America had through much of 2009 without context: 47 million Americans uninsured, $1.6 trillion over ten years, 17 percent of our economy spent on health care, some of the best cancer survival rates in the world, more spent on health care in the United States than any other country. I could go on and on, but you get the idea. Imagine trying to process all of those facts and arguments without any context. How would you ever come to sound conclusions about what we should do as a nation on this important issue if you didn't understand all the things that had happened already and that might happen in the future?

Let's just say it wouldn't be easy.

So why is context so important? Why does it really matter when you've got all the facts and figures? If America needs to spend X trillion dollars to fix health care, that's just the way it is, right? If a certain mutual fund had an X percent return last year, why can't you just say that and be done with it?

The answer is simple: without context, specifics are allowed to speak for themselves. The problem is, when you're not doing the speaking for them, your listener has much more freedom to do with those specifics as she pleases. In the absence of context to make the specifics make sense, her mind can immediately run wild with judgments, assumptions, and conclusions about what you've said that, more likely than not, are either plain wrong or shockingly off base.

For the sake of argument, let's say you're trying to sell MP3 players. Your new model is sleek, affordable, and has 8 gigabytes (GB) of memory. Now let's say you're talking to a mom who's interested in getting one of these for her son, but she doesn't know much about MP3 players, though she's quite comfortable with computers in general (her husband is in IT). Unless she's done a bit of research beforehand and has looked around, your claim that the MP3 player has 8GB of memory doesn't do much for her. The laptop she just bought her son for college has 120GB of memory and was only $500. And you're asking $200 for something with only a small fraction of that. No wonder she's not impressed: she thinks she's getting ripped off!

But what if, during the course of the conversation, you explain to her that MP3 players are different than laptops and require much less memory because song files aren't very big. And that, in fact, her son could fit hundreds of hours of music on this player, which is probably more than he has to begin with. You also explain that, for the price, it's a good amount of memory relative to other models, and really, it has a lot more memory than many of its competitors.

There's no way to be certain, but she just might buy it. The reason why? You've put the product and its features in context. On their own, 8GB of memory and a $200 price tag don't mean much to someone who isn't versed in the product, even if to you it's clear as day what a great deal it is. And assuming she's a skeptic like almost everyone she knows, she's not just going to pony up the money because it's the first MP3 player she comes across.

By putting the product in context, you've made the features make sense. You've given her more information, built more trust, and put her in control. You've given her the information she needs to feel good about the purchase. In fact, you could even invite her to go a step further and look around at all the different models to see that what you're saying is true.

In essence, you're helping her take a step back from the screen so the pixels make a picture that she can appreciate. And it is this crucial step of providing context that often makes or breaks how the specifics of your plan, product, or policy are received.

If the idea that how you state facts in certain ways can influence people's responses sounds familiar, it's because the idea has been around for quite some time. Marketers talk about putting benefits before features. Psychologists call it "priming." And in the political world we call it "framing."

What is important to remember is that every time you put forward new information, you must do so in a way that makes your information the most sensible in terms of the narrative you're trying to create. You must give it context, or frame it if you prefer the term, every time.

Not surprisingly, the academic work on creating context and framing leads us to the same conclusion: When you present the same information in different ways, different people interpret it how they see fit. Two social scientists tested and proved this theory in a 1981 study titled, "The Framing of Decisions and the Psychology of Choice." Amos Tversky and Daniel Kahneman demonstrated systematic reversals of preference when the same problem is presented in different ways, for example, in the Asian disease problem. Participants were asked to "imagine that the United States is preparing for the outbreak of an unusual Asian disease, which is expected to kill six hundred people. Two alternative programs to combat the disease have been proposed. Assume the exact scientific estimate of the consequences of the programs are as follows."

The first group of participants were presented with a choice between two programs:

Program A: "Two hundred people will be saved."
Program B: "There is a one-third probability that six hundred people will be saved, and a two-thirds probability that no people will be saved."

Seventy-two percent of participants preferred program A (the remainder, 28 percent, opted for program B). The second group of participants was presented with the choice between:

Program C: "Four hundred people will die."
Program D: "There is a one-third probability that nobody will die, and a two-thirds probability that six hundred people will die."

In this decision frame, 78 percent preferred program D, with the remaining 22 percent opting for program C. Programs A and C are identical, as are programs B and D. The change in the decision frame (from the number saved to the number who will die) between the two groups of participants produced a complete preference reversal. When framed in the context of the number of people that will be saved, three out of four people chose the program with the certain result ("Two hundred will be saved"). But when framed in the context of how many people will die, only about one in five chose the certain result ("Four hundred people will die").

Yeah, I had to read that about five times to get it all, too. In layman's terms, what it says is that depending on how you ask a question, people's responses can change dramatically even when you're basically asking the exact same thing. So your task as a communicator becomes choosing the right context in which to present your arguments, facts, and figures to make them as strong and convincing as possible.

A great professor of mine once said, "Everything vague will be interpreted negatively." She couldn't have been more right. Whether you are talking to your customers, your employees, the general public, or even your kids, vague statements will be interpreted in the way that best suits the listener. In the PTE, where you are guilty until proven innocent, that means that facts and statements will be construed in ways that work against you . . . unless you place them in the proper context. By creating the right context, you can sidestep this suspicion of guilt and build trust. And ultimately, that's what this is really all about.

Taken Out of Context

Where Communicators Go Wrong

There are many communicators I work with who are convinced that their salvation in the fight against their critics lies in "just getting the facts out there." Like Joe Friday from *Dragnet*, they want the conversation to be about facts rather than emotions because they believe that in a rational world, their position is more likely to prevail.

The problem with facts is that, well, there are simply too many of them. There are too many ways to communicate about a given event, product, or issue—all of them factual. We can use relative versus absolute numbers, limited versus broad time periods, or subsets of information rather than giving all of the information available. These tricks have probably been around since the dawn of time ("I'm only using a corner of your cave," meaning I left a sixteenth of the cave space open for you).

The late Benjamin Disraeli once said, "There are three kinds of lies: lies, damned lies, and statistics." To that I will add my own quote: "There is a statistic to support every opinion and a fact to prove every position." We see the battle of the facts go on every day in the great public opinion battles in Washington. Everyone has their fact sheets, and all of them are, at a purely factual level, accurate.

Imagine you are in the midst of a heated debate about whether or not a new cancer medication should be approved for sale by the FDA. Here are three facts about a clinical trial for a medication.

1. Patients were 300 percent more likely to die when taking the medication.

2. The death rate is 0.003 percent.

3. Three people died in the trial.

Should the medication be approved or never see the light of day? All three of these data points are based on the same fact. So they should all lead us to the same conclusion. But chances are fact 1 made you think this was a terrible drug, fact 2 made you think that this seems like a small risk for an important medication. And fact 3 doesn't tell you a whole lot of anything unless you believe that companies should never be allowed to develop new medications if even one life is at risk.

In the past, companies and politicians could get away with shading the truth and presenting their version of the facts. In the PTE, the challenge is much harder. Skeptics love a good unqualified fact or statistic—they love to tear it to pieces. They can smell the difference between information and spin—and the Internet and your competitors are more than ready to assist them.

This is the land where you shouldn't try this at home, you should consult your doctor first, you may experience a variety of side effects, and your mileage may vary. Once upon a time we all listened to the big picture and ignored the fine print—as manufacturers hoped we would—but today, we have become sensitized to it. We pay attention. And oftentimes, we seek out the fine print on our own, looking for it under a secret flap in the product instruction manual. No advertising slogan, product statement, or customer testimonial goes unquestioned. No fact is sacred. After all, 73 percent of facts are made up on the spot . . . right? Without context, facts, statistics, and specific details about your product or company are just numbers.

Today, communicators fail when they ignore the importance of context. If you don't give your audience the bigger picture, they will fill it in for you. They will assume you are leaving out the negative contextual details of your message, not the positive. After all, leaving out context has traditionally been one of the most common forms of disinformation in sales, politics, and other areas:

Without Context	With Context
Our product lasts longer.	It has a slightly lower failure rate, but these failures result in much higher than average repair bills.
This investment has the highest guaranteed rate of return.	A whole big, fat eighth of a point higher—this week, anyway.
My opponent voted for higher taxes forty-two times.	Most of these votes were for routine budget bills with a mixture of tax cuts and increases.
I have strong opinions.	I often get fired for insubordination.

Ever heard statements like these? Did you doubt them? More important, have you considered making statements like these about your product, idea, company, or yourself? If you have, think through what you would say about each if you were questioned about them in detail. Then decide if they are still worth saying with the full weight of context behind them.

Consider oil companies talking about alternative energy sources. Leaders in oil production are wearing themselves out talking about their investments in greener production practices, biofuels made with everything from algae to fish oil, and research projects that could lead to better, cleaner energy sources. Imagine a hypothetical oil giant—we'll call them Global Oil—wants to talk about its efforts to produce clean algae-based biofuel. After all, it is making big investments, and it would like to get some credit. It proudly states that it will be spending $40 million on biofuel technology over the next ten years. It says it is a leader in the green energy revolution.

It is here, at this point in the conversation, that context comes in. If Global Oil signs off, ends its commercial, or hits "send" on the press release after making these simple statements, then it is losing its battle to the skeptics. And for good reason. It is leaving out context—both good and bad. Consumers who are already suspicious of big oil companies—big anything companies, for that matter—will immediately start questioning Global Oil's motives. Where exactly is that money going? How much is it compared with the amount it is spending drilling for oil? And the big kahuna of questions: what kind of piddly, little investment is $40 million for a company that rakes in such high profits? Spending $4 million a year on clean energy while you make $40 *billion* on "dirty" oil is hardly something to write home about.

Unfortunately, context is one area where your gut instincts usually fail you. It is in our nature to shade meaning in our favor and spare people bad news. Think of a child coming home from school to tell her parents she got the best grade in math this semester. She leaves out the fact that none of her grades were above a C. Or consider a husband coming home from a job interview, explaining to his wife that he thought things went very well. He doesn't explain that there are fifty-seven other qualified candidates interviewing for the position. Then there is the racer who proudly proclaims he came in second while leaving out the minor detail that there were only two people in the race. We naturally leave context out when we feel it is not in our best interest.

My work has shown that following this instinct is usually not the right course. Time and time again, we have shown in Instant Response dial sessions that providing context, even when that framing is not completely positive, is the surest path to building trust. Done correctly, providing context—or framing your message—can help you regain trust in the PTE.

Let's go back to Global Oil. It believes that it has a story to tell. It thought that it could communicate that its $40 million was an example of it doing the right thing. It was wrong. Now suppose it tells more of its story and provides greater information about how this investment fits into its larger corporate narrative. Maybe $40 million is the most any major oil company has ever spent on biofuel technology, or perhaps it is twice the amount the company is spending on finding new sources of crude oil. Maybe it will provide jobs for hundreds of people in a part of the United States that has been particularly devastated by the economy or outsourcing of jobs. And maybe the $40 million is just one part or just the first part of a larger commitment to alternative energy. Of course, there will be skeptics out there who say that it will never be enough until the company stops selling oil. But for many others—including many otherwise skeptical people—this context will ensure that Global Oil's $40 million investment doesn't end up doing it more reputational harm than good.

As you can see from this example, there are many ways to place facts into context. We compared Global to its peers and to its own other business units. We put it in the context of jobs and the economy. And we placed it into a larger corporate narrative around the company's commitment. Each of these can help explain and thereby build trust. There are no strict rules on how you must build your message to create an effective context. There are, however, three overarching approaches to set the context:

- Context explains actions.

- Context provides perspective.

- Context sets expectations.

In every case, there will be some overlap: by providing perspective you can also explain your actions, and so on. The key here is using context to your advantage rather than allowing your facts and specifics to be used against you.

Context Explains Actions

All of us have been on flights when the flight attendant asks the passengers to buckle seat belts, lock tray tables, and put seats in their upright position. We have all been asked to stay seated or to refrain from using portable electronics. We have been asked not to form a line near the forward lavatory. In fact, we can probably recite these commands in our sleep. We do these things not just because our safety is at stake, but because it is required. And they aren't really asking, are they? We know that it is "Federal Aviation Guidelines" that state that no one under the age of thirteen can sit in an exit row . . . yada, yada, yada. We require no context because there is no option to decline—no opportunity to walk away.

Now consider if that same flight attendant asks more than what is required. What if, for instance, she asks you to pick up the trash around your seat or to close your window shade after landing? You really have no real obligation to do these things—besides common courtesy. So how do they get you to do it? They provide context. They give you the "why."

JetBlue was the first airline I remember to ask people to clean up after themselves, and it was successful because it did just that. It explained that when a few flight attendants were left to clean an entire cabin, it took them a long time and could sometimes even cause delays. The airline said that extra help on board cost extra money. So if you could just pick up your old magazine and pretzel wrapper, you would ultimately be saving yourself both time and money. The subtext was not, "you're a lazy slob," it was, "you're a smart traveler." Who doesn't want to save money or avoid delays?

Other airlines have asked passengers to close shades before deplaning, because—again—it will save them money. Lowered shades result in a cooler plane. A cooler plane requires less fuel to keep the temperature regulated. And less fuel use should mean lower ticket costs. Not to mention, it's not so bad for the environment either.

In both of these cases, context provides reasoning for actions. It fills in the background information the audience needs to make a decision—in this case, a decision to help out the flight attendants. By giving them the "why" and explaining what's in it for them, you gain trust. Now, whether picking up a few bits of paper or shutting some shades saves a significant amount of money remains to be seen, but the point is passengers are willing to help out when they have a reason to do so.

Context can also explain the actions of individuals, not just corporations. Imagine you are interviewing a candidate—John Doe—for a position at your firm, and his résumé sports a large "gap" (in layman terms—or for anyone who has somehow avoided reading résumé tips—this is a time period with no employment history listed). You—being a true skeptic—immediately assume this guy can't keep a job or, worse, is just plain lazy. You begin to cross your arms and zone out. Luckily for John, he has taken a few tips from this book. The conversation goes something like this:

> **You:** So I see that you have some gaps in your employment history. Can you tell me what happened there?
>
> **John:** Well, that's actually a really good question. My wife and I decided one of us should stay home with our child after he was born so that we could limit his time spent in day care. I volunteered, and I took the opportunity to brush up on my professional certifications. I actually was able to earn my Six Sigma Black Belt during that time, so it worked out for me—and my last employer.

Ooooh. Ahhhh. You suddenly find yourself first in line to hire John, because he was able to provide context that explained his actions. He gave you the bad information (time out of work) with the good (bonus certifications), and gained your trust as a result.

Context in Internal Communication

One of the places where effective and credible communications makes the most significant difference is in the world of internal communications. Whether you are in a small business or a large one, there are often critical moments in time where the company's words actually speak louder than the actions themselves. In other words, certain actions are viewed as a sign of great management or serious ineptitude based exclusively on how and when the actions are communicated. I have seen this up close in a number of companies over the past few years in the midst—and aftermath—of major restructurings or layoffs. It is at these moments that management must communicate effectively or years of trust building can be erased in a matter of days.

Not surprisingly, the first thing employees want to know about in the face of a major announcement is, "What is happening to me, today"? "Do I still have a job?" These are questions of personal survival, not corporate morale. If you are fired, your morale is not terribly important to the company after all. Once employees know they are still on the team, however, the challenge is to communicate to them what happened and why it happened in a way that keeps them engaged and motivated as employees.

And here is where it gets interesting. At this point, you might think that people want to know the details of the actions—the facts, figures, and statistics. But this is actually pretty low on their priority list. Instead, what they want next is what we call "understanding"—employees want to understand the larger rationale behind what the company is doing. They want context. This isn't about the company's vision; they can't think about the future yet. What they want is to understand why the company made the decisions it did and what criteria they used to decide the specifics.

In one project for a major global company, we found that management had lost a great deal of credibility in the aftermath of layoffs. The employees actually supported the layoffs because they recognized that the company was bloated and bureaucratic. But they blamed management for failing to articulate the criteria that was used to decide why one of their work colleagues was terminated while someone who appeared to be less competent was still employed. By not setting the context of the actions they were taking, employees assumed the worst—that it was all political—and their perceptions of management suffered as a result.

Context Provides Perspective

In the past few years, cosmetic and personal care companies have come under fire for the use of parabens in their products. In fact, parabens can be found in everything from lipstick to baby lotion. So what are they? They sound pretty scary, huh? Like something you might want to avoid? Now consider what parabens do: they are preservatives that prevent your products from becoming infected by bacteria. So what sounds scarier now: parabens in your eyeliner or bacteria growing on your mascara wand?

Even armed with this information, some skeptical consumers still won't be convinced; they would still prefer products with as few additives as possible. After all, natural is always better, right? Communicators talking about parabens could go one step further, creating context by offering additional information. They could explain that these preservatives actually occur naturally in common foods we eat, like blueberries and peas. Parabens are a safe, natural ingredient that keeps your cosmetic products safe. Now what do you think? Still scary? Our research shows that, at this point, we have your attention. You are less concerned about the "scary" ingredient, and are ready to focus on the other benefits of the product.

Providing some perspective can make your audience more comfortable with whatever idea you are selling. More comfortable with your product, its ingredients, or the way it's manufactured. Often by providing additional information, or clarification, you give people a reason to believe you—you regain the benefit of the doubt. And in the PTE, that small advantage can help you continue the conversation with your consumer and, hopefully, make the sale.

We know that skeptics frequently go online and do their own research about products. They go to Google, Wikipedia, and blogs written by people around the world. Moms blog about baby products. Athletes blog about gym equipment. Students blog about courses and professors. So much information is available that your audience begins to have trouble wading through it all. It becomes more difficult for them to distinguish flowery sales techniques and hyperbole from honest statements. Unqualified facts and information from you—facts and information without context to give perspective—become part of the noise. In order to break through, you must offer more than just information, you must offer perspective. By doing so, you can often help clear the air around an issue.

Take an example from my firm's work within the dairy industry. If you Google "IGF-1," you will find an incredibly diverse collection of data, blog entries, scientific articles, and personal stories. You would find that IGF-1 is a chemical present in milk and other dairy products. You would also find articles about IGF-1 being discovered in biopsies of tumors. You would see many claims linking this chemical to cancer.

For milk producers, this presents a real problem. Talk to them and they reject the notion that IGF-1 as present in their products is harmful. They drink the products. They feed it to their children. They drink it while they are pregnant. But they fear, rightfully, that consumers don't trust them when they say that IGF-1 is safe. So how do they have a conversation about IGF-1 to present their side of the story and help divert a potential customer relations disaster? My firm talked to hundreds of milk consumers around the country, and we found that by providing a little perspective, the issue becomes . . . well, a nonissue. Consider this background information:

While it is true that IGF-1 has been found in tumors, this is consistent with the fact that IGF-1 is produced naturally in the human body. The average person naturally produces more IGF-1 each day than you would consume if you drank gallons and gallons of milk.

Now the picture changes from a PR professional's nightmare to a case of lost perspective. While some skeptics will still doubt the truth of a statement like this, they can get back on Google or Wikipedia, or go to the FDA's or the National Institutes of Health's websites, and confirm the information.

The fact is, facts alone can be misleading. Information about your company or product that appears negative, given the proper perspective, can be neutralized.

Unfortunately, the same principle also works for positive facts, and is especially relevant when it comes to the complicated statistics or expert data you use to promote yourself or your product. Yes, it's true. Yes, it makes you look good. The problem is, your audience doesn't understand it. They're not less clever or less intuitive than you; they simply require context to make sense of the information.

Let's consider a consumer at his local market, searching for food that has the lowest impact on the environment. This buyer drives a Prius sporting a "Hide-Free" bumper sticker, he lives in a house built primarily from recycled and found materials, and he shops at Whole Foods and local markets like this one. He gets to the breakfast aisle and is faced with a choice of two wheat flake cereal boxes, each labeled "environmentally sustainable." Each uses a new, innovative technique to grow the grains that go into the product. The first says, "The new process used to grow these grains results in a 7 percent reduction of environmental impact per box." The second says,

"Using this new farming process in just 20 percent of U.S. wheat fields has the same impact as taking 500,000 cars off the road each year." Which do you think he buys? Which would you buy?

Both of these labels are saying the exact same thing—they are offering a positive fact about the sustainability of the product. The first, however, gives a percentage—of an unknown, unidentified amount—for which the consumer has no understanding. How big is 7 percent? Is that a lot? A little? The consumer is not stupid or uninformed, he just has no perspective. The second label, however, gives the same information in terms of cars off the road—an environmental impact the consumer can visualize. How big is that impact? It's a half million cars big. By giving context to your positive facts, you can give your audience much-needed perspective on the issue.

Context can also provide the perspective you need to break through your audience's personal filters. Each of us filters what we hear through our own lenses—our culture, our personality, our wealth, our age, and other factors. We filter out the messages that don't apply to us, and let in the messages that do. For example, high-net worth individuals need more specific background data than other individuals before making investment decisions. Invesco has described this filter as "whealthy skepticism." In order to reach this group, financial advisors must provide enough information—historical data, graphs, relevant statistics—to break through. Addressing broader factors influenced by these filters—security for an older investor, or growth potential for a younger one—builds credibility and trust. Learning to provide context from within the consumer's own mind-set is critical to communicating today.

Take the twentysomething who has just joined the workforce. Talking about saving for a secure retirement isn't very relevant to her: retirement seems like it is a million years away. Same with income growth potential. She will filter out this "useless" information—she is probably more worried about making her next car payment or paying off her student loans. But you can harness the power of her personal mind-set—her filter—by giving her the right information. Don't just talk about compounding interest; show her what it means by providing context and perspective:

> **Advisor:** Did you know that if one person invests $2,000 a year from age twenty to thirty, and then never invests again, she will accumulate more money for retirement than someone who invests the same amount every year from age thirty to age sixty-five?

Everyone knows that money grows with interest, but few people understand how time presents an opportunity for young people to put their future on autopilot. While retirement itself may not be a hot button for this young person, not having to put her nose to the grindstone for most of her adult life just might be. Thinking issues through from the customer's perspective—particularly if you ask the right questions—can open up new ways of providing context.

Conversely, knowing your audience prevents you from leading with contexts that are hot buttons for people. Married women don't like being categorized as earning second incomes, particularly when they are doctors and CEOs. Mature high–net worth individuals who have lived through one Great Depression and fear another don't trust your promises of safety—they want to hear about diversification instead. And in the financial markets that followed the crash of 2008, fewer people than ever think of themselves as "investors."

Saving the Environment . . . Up to a Point

Ask Californians whether they support more renewable energy, and the answer is a resounding yes. Ask them if they want the government to set higher and higher goals for utilities to meet and they will raise their hands. Ask them if they think that utilities should be prohibited from building new power plants if they cause pollution and they will stand up and clap.

Then ask them whether they are willing to pay significantly higher rates necessary to cover the cost of building solar and wind power facilities and some will sit down again. Or ask them if they are willing to accept rolling blackouts at night when the sun doesn't shine and the enthusiasm will start to leave the room.

The difference then between unequivocal support for the shift to renewable energy and a much more cautious approach depends entirely on the context into which we place the discussion. If we focus solely on environmental goals, there is no end to support. If we place the environment in the broader context of reliable electricity, affordable electricity, and clean and sustainable electricity, then the situation is different. The context provides perspective. The perspective creates an inevitable set of trade-offs. And amidst those trade-offs people are able to evaluate what is most important for them.

Without the broader context, the utility is forced to oppose environmental initiatives and be demonized as a result. Within this context, however, utilities can communicate their support for the right environmental initiatives that promote cleaner, renewable energy without sacrificing reliability or making electricity too expensive for consumers.

Context Sets Expectations

Context gives you an opportunity to reframe a conversation—even one leading down a potentially negative path—by setting expectations. When you talk about your company performance, for example, you can compare yourself either to a small group of company peers or a larger group of companies in your and related industries. You can compare your performance to last year or to the goals that you set out at the beginning of the year. Perhaps your stock is lagging behind the market, but is doing tremendously well compared to your internal predictions. In context, a bad situation (low stock earnings) can actually be an okay thing (exceeding goals).

Consider two high school graduates applying for college admission. The university has a blind admission process, and considers only the candidates' high school transcripts as criteria for their decision. Applicant A earned average grades in all classes, has an SAT score that just meets university admission standards, and was ranked fiftieth in the class. Applicant B made excellent grades, has a strong SAT score, and was ranked second in the class. Which would you admit? The obvious choice is Applicant B.

Now imagine the same two applicants have applied to a second school. This college allows them to present context (read: personal essays and interviews) along with their transcripts. Applicant A is actually Nathan, one of four hundred graduates from his class at a top-tier magnet high school. His school offered eight Advanced Placement courses and four foreign languages, and Nathan took advantage of each one! He participated in many extracurricular activities, and placed highly in a national science contest. Applicant B is Julie, who attended a private high school and graduated with thirty-two other students. She took only one Advanced Placement course, and supplemented that with easier classes like Taking Picnics 101 and Underwater Basket-Weaving for Beginners. She chose not to participate in any clubs or organizations in her free time.

Now who would you admit to your university? Nathan, the well-rounded science champ, or Julie, the chronic underachiever? When the candidates were compared in a vacuum, the admission decision seemed simple and obvious. Given context to set expectations for each applicant, the result is entirely different. The admissions officer at the first school might have been skeptical of choosing Applicant A over the "more qualified" Applicant B, but would have reconsidered if all the cards were on the table.

Of course, this is a very simplistic example—not to mention one that you probably won't run into unless you're hoping to be part of the graduating college class of 2014. So, how can real people—real communicators—use context to set customer expectations? Or, more important, how can you set expectations to change the context in which your audience sees you?

One of our clients, a mortgage company, asked us to explore the customer service relationship. Specifically, they wanted to better understand how to more effectively communicate with chronic late payers. For the business, it was critical to engage these customers to avoid going to the bottom of the customer's list of creditors. For the customer, it was just another painful phone call from a company trying to wring money from their limited savings. So how could this call be different? The answer was actually fairly simple: change the context. Most collection calls are just that: calls to collect a debt. The creditor gets on the phone and talks about the specific amounts owed and challenges the customer to make a payment or come up with a payment plan. The call is adversarial in nature, even when the caller uses a friendly tone. But the problem for most people with late payments is not a lack of desire to pay; it is a lack of ability. They are faced with a situation where they need to juggle different creditors and decide which is first.

We found that there were two key ingredients necessary to change the context of the conversation. The first step was to move from adversary to partner by finding a common goal. In this case it was also important to acknowledge the customers' biggest fear: losing their home. The second step was to change the goal of the conversation by providing a new context for the call. Instead of calling to collect money, we framed the conversation as one in which the mortgage company was seeking to get the customer back on track with his or her payments.

An Approach That Works

"We're in the business of helping you to get things taken care of. We're not in the business of taking your home.

The purpose of my call is to work with you to get your payments up-to-date. There are a lot of options that we can explore to help you get things back on track."

This change of context changed expectations—both for the mortgage company and their customers. On one side, the company's message was no longer framed by the need for immediate payment. Instead, it was an understanding that a payment schedule would be established. At the same time, customers no longer felt bullied and pressured. They still realized that paying back the mortgage was necessary, but they were given options. What we heard from customers was a greater openness to the conversation; a greater willingness to discuss the reasons for failing to make payments; and, ultimately, a higher likelihood of payment.

Providing—or changing—the context of your message allows you to set expectations for the conversation that follows. It's not just about matching the benchmark or meeting the industry standard; it's about your specific goals, your particular situation, and your personal contribution. What's more, when you set expectations appropriately, the discussion naturally reverts back to the most important part of the conversation: your customer.

Context in Action: Language Lenses

Identifying the right context for an issue or a product is a critical part of what my company and I do to understand how best to communicate our client's position. We have engaged the audience, and we have identified their interests and acknowledged their concerns and issues. It is at this point that we want to communicate our client's position—why to buy its product or agree with it on its issue. Our objective is to ensure that the audience is open and willing to listen to our client's perspective and that the message is received and interpreted in the manner intended by the client. To do this we begin to explore different frames for communicating about the issue.

Let's take a part of the health care debate. Medicare Part D has been an extremely controversial piece of legislation since it was passed. Perhaps the most controversial element of it has been the prohibition of direct negotiation between the government and pharmaceutical companies on drug prices. Under current legislation, the individual insurance companies negotiate drug prices rather than the federal government. Opponents of this legislation argue that drug prices would come down much more quickly if the government could use the fact that it insures millions of patients as leverage to negotiate with the drug companies. Our client asked us to argue the other side. Below is a list of just four of the nearly twenty frames we developed as well as an example of how we developed both a positive message and a negative message for each frame. Each of the approaches is based on the industry's—and many independent

Frame	Positive Message	Negative Message
Choice	Current Part D provides a wide range of drug coverage and pricing choices.	Government negotiation would cut down on coverage and pricing choices.
	"This is about personal choice and finding the plan that works best for each senior."	"One-size-fits-some Medicare."
Control	Current Part D puts seniors in control of their health care.	Government negotiation would reduce control for seniors.
	"Seniors, and their doctors, should control which medications they take."	"Government-controlled health care."
Price and Affordability	Current Part D is an effective tool to lower prices for seniors.	Government negotiation would not result in significant added savings.
	"Most seniors are already paying the least they have ever paid for prescription medications."	"Price fixing, not negotiation."
Politics (Campaign Issues)	Current Part D takes politics *out* of the drug pricing equation.	Government negotiation is good politics but bad policy.
	"Depoliticizing Medicare."	"Raising expectations more than lowering prices."

experts'—opinion of the likely impact of a change in policy. Our job was to find the approach among many options and arguments that would be most persuasive.

Each of these messages is supported by proof points, or facts (such as they are), and then tested: for understanding and clarity, for believability, and for persuasiveness. The results help us to decide how best to approach the issue with the target audience.

Putting Trust in Context

The section you have just read may prove to be the most controversial in this book. After all, I spent much of the book talking about trust and then the last few sections showing you how to influence the way people interpret facts. These are the things that DC has been doing for the last decade or more to erode trust in America, right?

The simple answer is yes. These are the same tactics used to create some of the more well-known turns of phrase in politics and campaigns. We live in a world of information on demand. If your story has another side, it is only a mouse click away. That means it is *your* job to provide the context for your story rather than allowing it to be filled in by your competitors or adversaries.

The process of selling products, services, and ideas has moved in a totally different direction, from the one-sided approach of the salesman to the customer advocate and educational resource of the trusted communicator. Be the first to speak the language, and you will be the first to gain the trust and respect of the skeptical consumer. Come late to the party, and you will have an uphill battle selling in the future. This new generation of trust seeking has added a completely new dimension to what public relations professionals have told us for years: context is everything.

PART FOUR

THE MEDIUM
AND
THE MESSAGE

Much of the work I do requires more than research to develop and test messages for my clients. In some ways the research is the easy part. The harder part is applying the messages to real-world situations, where there is always a seemingly good reason to ignore the lessons in this book. For example, I have found many clients (like many politicians) are perfectly happy to stay positive until they are hit hard with a critic's attack. Then the typical response is that they can't leave such an attack unanswered. And they go negative. In other situations, clients argue that their customers don't have time to listen to context; they just want the facts. And so they provide a litany of facts and can't understand why sales don't improve. In practice, some of the recommendations I make in this book will be uncomfortable and challenging. I can only say that in project after project, our clients who implement them talk about how using language to build trust does help them persuade people who are otherwise skeptical to buy what they are selling.

The purpose of these final chapters is not to add to the language of trust. Hopefully, the most important elements of using language to overcome skepticism have been clearly outlined already. Instead, this part of the book includes two chapters with two different goals but a common theme of putting the language of trust into practice.

The first chapter is about applying the language of trust in a digital world. It is impossible to ignore how digital communication has changed our approach to selling, marketing, and protecting our reputation. In many ways, digital media have changed the nature of the conversation. But communication is still communication. The strategies are different, as are the opportunities and risks, but the core elements of what you say and how you say it generally stay the same. After all, in a digital world, one of the most important rules is that you keep your message consistent, because inconsistencies will be found and used against you. That rule holds true from online to offline communications as well, suggesting that you really can only have one message—one communicated in the language of trust. So the next chapter will walk you through how digital media affect the process of building credibility and what you as a communicator can do to take advantage of the incredible opportunities to better engage and persuade your audience.

The final chapter we have compiled is a list of what not to say. As I said earlier, it is often what you eliminate from your lexicon that has the greatest positive impact on how you are perceived. If trust can be broken in a misplaced phrase, then removing the credibility killers from your communication is often the first step in reassessing how you communicate. We have identified seven "anti-trust laws"—categories of statements that you should avoid at all costs. We have also included twenty banned phrases that illustrate what we mean by each anti-trust law. Not only do I hope you ban the specific phrases, but I hope they help you to avoid creating new ones that fall into the same traps.

10

The Language of
Trust in a Digital World

You've probably noticed that communicating in 2010 is a little different than it used to be. If you have kids, you may even worry that their thumbs are going to fall off or their heads are going to get stuck permanently looking down from so much texting, IMing, and constant connection. Every day the dividing line between the online world and the offline world is shrinking. While we're watching YouTube videos on our laptops, the TV networks pick up stories first printed on blogs like Politico or Perez Hilton or "breaking news tweets" flying around on Twitter. Tiny tweets link to long, in-depth blog posts, which differ from newspaper op-eds more in tone and length than pure substance. And most important, nothing of significance to customers or the public ever stays entirely in one world or the other.

With the world of social media, iPhone apps, blogging, and even email and websites looking so different than traditional offline modes of communicating, it's completely reasonable to ask if this new world of constant connection requires a different approach to using language to build trust. As more and more clients recognize the power of social media and the web (if you haven't recognized this, then you have bigger problems than the message), this question is becoming increasingly common.

I'll confess here that I am not a digital media expert. I can't talk about the technologies that will allow you to master the art of engaging your audience online with cool apps or a masterful social media strategy. What I can say is that I have studied how leading, effective communicators are using digital strategies to build trust through messaging. And what I can tell you is that the strategies for communicating with audiences online through media such as blogs and websites aren't starkly different than the strategies for communicating through more traditional means. You just have to understand the nuances and why communicating in the digital world is so important.

I have also enlisted the help of a friend and corporate digital strategist named Peter Hirsch to identify the most important differences between the online and offline world as well as a series of seven approaches for overcoming skepticism online that differ from the way we approach communicating offline. Peter has been on the front lines with companies executing communication strategies for more than fifteen years and was early to recognize the importance of digital strategies for companies trying to get their message out.

The Differences

Just because the nature of communication in the online world is different from what happens offline, that doesn't mean you need two different strategies for communicating effectively in either. Instead, the crossover between offline and online communication means you need to understand both worlds so you can develop a messaging strategy that will allow you to succeed in both. Below are some of the key differences that communicators now must account for when developing any message strategy.

Outrage spreads virally ... but the virus often ends up being a twenty-four-hour bug. In the offline world, it actually takes work for critics to say something bad about a company, a person, or a product. What's more, even in the days of the twenty-four-hour news cycle, you still had to go looking for it: you had to turn on the TV, find the pundits, buy the paper, and so on. But in the online world, you can tell hundreds of people (or more) about your experience in thirty seconds. And if you do a good job, your criticism will be passed happily along thanks to a circulation culture that rewards those who redistribute. Rather than having to go out and look for more information, critiques, or arguments, they all come to you thanks to email updates, text alerts, RSS feeds, and blogs updated by the minute. Gathering information about what's going on in a company or around the world has become more passive than it used to be. Our new level of technological proficiency has removed the need to scour different sources for things we care about or things that interest us. Any topic, any commentator, any story can be delivered to us on demand before a newspaper can even dream about getting to press.

This new, lower bar for online activism and engagement means that outrage spreads virally with incredible speed. In a matter of minutes, a small problem can become a big problem, which can then escalate into a full-blown crisis and make it feel like the sky is falling.

There is an equally important flip side. The low bar for activism also means that much of this outrage is superficial and, more important, fleeting. Much like a school of fish that swerves in unison, the digital population is quick to move to the next place where they can voice their opinions and move on.

This poses a significant challenge for companies trying to judge how to react to an attack on their products or reputation. Do you react swiftly to mitigate the damage? Or wait out the firestorm until there is another, better target for people to move on to? The unfortunate answer is: it depends. While you should always react (see the box on page 95), the nature of your reaction must depend on whether you are dealing with a twenty-four-hour bug or full-blown swine flu.

Gauging Outrage

We all say the wrong thing sometimes. But today a perceived slight can get fueled by the high octane of social media and spread quickly around the nation.

When Johnson & Johnson launched an advertising campaign aimed at mothers for its popular pain reliever Motrin, they put out what they thought was a lighthearted take on the practice of "baby wearing." A video ad on their website talked about how it "seems to be in fashion" to carry your kid and how it "supposedly" was a bonding experience— and then went on to imply that it caused aches and pains that, of course, Motrin could take care of.

This ad quickly raised a firestorm of protest from mothers who found it snarky and patronizing, not to mention inaccurate: for example, some pointed out that people have been wearing their babies for hundreds of years, not just recently, and that it wasn't a guaranteed ticket for back pain when done properly.

Above all, many resented the implication that they were carrying their babies to be fashionable or, as the ad put it, an "official mom." And since today's moms are highly connected, they weren't shy about posting their opinions on their blogs and Twitter feeds, and soon the viral spread of this controversy made it a major news story.

But here is the real irony of this flap: In a subsequent study, a majority of women surveyed either liked the ad or had no feelings about it; in fact, four times as many of them liked the brand better afterward than vice versa. But we all learned that even an annoyed minority can ignite a media crisis over the Internet if you touch a sensitive enough nerve. In the aftermath of this episode, Johnson & Johnson did all the right things: They pulled the ad, apologized, and spoke transparently about learning their lessons from an important market. Presumably, one of those lessons was to test-market future campaigns among those who tweet.[23]

You don't control the flow of information anymore . . . but you get much more information to use in crafting your strategy. As a company or organization trying to communicate a message, you've just outsourced your PR department to the wisdom of crowds. It's no longer about just what you say; it's what lots of people hear *and* what they say to each other. In my experience, most organizations still communicate as if they are the only source of "official information" out there. They create their messages as if they have a soapbox and an attentive audience. In reality, however, the language you use must acknowledge, either implicitly or explicitly, that you are only one source among many.

The good news is that as the crowds take control of the message, they are placing their own commentary around the issue, using their own language to redefine the debate, and giving you feedback about what matters most and why in the process. There is an Internet culture of "I have something to say and I'm going to say it" that gives us priceless insights into the minds of consumers—insights we could only have dreamed about getting just fifteen or twenty years ago. There are also great technologies out there—many of them free—that allow you to view and analyze the conversations as they happen. We can now anticipate and adapt our communication strategies much more quickly because we can see, in real time, what people are saying about us—the good, the bad, and the ugly.

You aren't as important in cyberspace as you think you are . . . and maybe not as important as the parent in pajamas. Not only have you lost the power to control the conversation (remember the good old days?), you are now competing for "share of voice," to use an industry term, with people you never, in your wildest dreams, thought of as competition. These aren't necessarily your competitors or your professional critics. Instead, it might be the typical man or woman in pajamas, sitting at home on a Saturday afternoon nursing a bowl of soggy cereal, who has built a following writing about your company or companies like it. And online, the size of your company, the value or your stock, and the amount of money you spend on advertising cannot buy you credibility or importance—you have to earn it. Contrary to what many companies are doing today, building a Facebook page isn't a strategy that will automatically ensure a following.

The Internet, like the pistol, has leveled the playing field. No matter how small or weak someone is, that person's voice can be heard and accessed just as easily as yours. Online you are an equal, no more powerful than the stay-at-home dad who took up the cause against you. You are no more (and maybe even less) credible than the woman in pajamas—both you and she have to earn the right to have an audience. Your tone and messaging need to reflect that if you want to get anyone to listen. And because you are likely trying to convince your audience to change their attitude about something, you have to work that much harder to anticipate their skepticism and address it in your message before it has a chance to derail you.

You can react much more quickly, but once you make a choice it is irrevocable. In addition to getting information to anticipate issues much more quickly, you can also react infinitely more quickly and less formally online than you can offline. Want to demonstrate that you are part of the conversation? A simple tweet can at least let the world know you are paying attention or can get people to see information that starts to tell your story. At a minimum, you can acknowledge the issue and let your audience know you will be back with a response shortly. For some issues, this simple acknowledgment can turn you from a tin-eared corporate behemoth to an organization that listens to its customers and (gasp!) cares. The beauty is that you can do all of this at no or very low cost, and you can even find ways to react to sensitive situations that don't require legions of lawyers and days of review.

Unfortunately, you also have to get your answer right the first time. Everything you say on the web is permanent, so you'd better be prepared to live with what you do. This shouldn't deter you from responding when you know you need to, but it is a fact of life. If you put it out there, it will never be fully erased from our digital memory. Bet on it. And what happens when you change it, and then try to act like you didn't? Someone produces a screen shot, posts it on a blog, and you look bad—really bad. Quick responses are often necessary and can stem the tide of anger from washing you out to sea, but you must be willing to stand behind what you put out there the first time.

Using the Language of Trust Online

As I said, the differences between the online and offline worlds do not require a new language for you or your company. Despite all the talk about us turning into a text-messaging culture, your message should be your message—whether you say it verbally or digitally. The worst thing you can do is get caught talking out of both sides of your mouth, especially if you get caught by the digital generation, which is already the most skeptical we've ever seen in American history.

With that as a starting point, here are seven things you can do with your messaging online to overcome skepticism and build trust with your audience online.

1. You do not have to tell your story in 140 characters. One of the biggest myths of the online world is that communicators have less time to communicate their message online than offline. Believe it or not, the opposite is actually true—once you engage a user, you have the opportunity to tell your whole story in a way that is unmatched by any other medium.

Now, it certainly is true that you can't tell your story if you can't get people to your site or blog. For that reason, it *is* necessary to master the art of engaging your audience in 140 characters or less. But is that any different than in any other medium (other than face-to-face)? Whether you are online, on TV, the radio, or in print, you have only a few seconds to grab your audience's attention. This has always been the case and isn't some new hurdle caused by LCD displays and 3G networks.

What's so great about online communication is that once you have their attention, online media give you a much higher level of engagement and much greater opportunity to tell your story in depth and, best of all, on your terms.

For example, in September 2009, Gmail went down for several long, painful hours. For anyone who relies on Gmail for business or personal reasons, this was a big deal. On every other medium but the web, Google's apology was or would have been relegated to a quote from the company explaining what had happened and offering a brief apology. That's because in every other medium, especially TV and radio, the rules of the road are simple: keep it short, sweet, and to the point so you don't get misquoted or taken out of context. The problem is, sometimes the point can't be put across in any meaningful way in just thirty seconds. So we get the watered-down, boilerplate version that just leaves everyone feeling kind of, well, pissed.

But on the web, Google could tell its story. And it did . . . in detail. More than a simple apology, they also acknowledged the significance of the event, detailed what had happened, and outlined their course of action to ensure it would never happen again. About five hundred words later, the reader had the complete story and an undeniable sense that Google was in control of the situation. Do you really think a fifty-word, thirty-second hit on a news program could have done the same thing?

Yes, that question was rhetorical.

2. Be a part of the conversation wherever you can be. As digital media expert Peter Hirsch says, "I used to think arguing on the Internet was like getting into an argument with a drunk at the bar—it was a fight you can't win. Now it is clear that you need to communicate. You can't leave it out there." True, you still might not be able to win, but you can at least put up a good fight. If someone is talking negatively about you online, there is no question that you have to respond. The level of response must vary relative to the size of the issue and the number of people with whom you are arguing, but the need for a response should not. Even more so than in the offline world, silence only hurts you in the complex world of blogs, forums, and social media. Silence cedes the floor to the opposition and lets them define the terms of the debate. Silence places no obstacles in front of the other side's momentum, making it easier for them to build steam. And silence gives your supporters nothing to grab onto to communicate their support. Put simply, if you are asking yourself whether you should comment, the answer is yes. And the time to do so is now.

3. **Linking and navigating is part of your message.** On the web, your message is much larger than what you are saying about your company. Just as critics are saying negative things about you, others are saying good things about you or at least providing the kind of information that you would like more people to know about. In the offline world, it is often a difficult process to get a third party to act as a proxy to disseminate your message. But online, it simply requires a little bit of HTML to connect your message to the messages of others who are already out there supporting you.

Online, you have the ability to use the medium to broaden the conversation in a way that helps you tell your story. In other words, your message is what *you* say plus everything that the sites to which you link say.

Think, for a moment, about how people use the web. Linking and searching drive how people navigate. Remember the last time you went to look up something on Wikipedia only to find yourself ten minutes later eighteen clicks in and five topics removed? People jump from site to site as they follow different leads or seek more information about a topic or a point of view. Now think about the old communication paradigm: Go promote your story in the face of other information. You either assume that the other information isn't known by your audience or that you can dictate the terms of the conversation by telling your story louder than the critics or the competition. The old paradigm no longer works because the opposing point of view is one search away. Remember, you can't really outshout or buy up all the ad time on the Internet. As a result, the only way to control the message is to acknowledge the broader conversation. Rather than only telling your side, you now must tell your side and show what the other side is saying through links and navigation on your site. By referencing the other points of view in the conversation, you build credibility (and trust) while also positioning your site as a trusted source for information on a given topic.

4. **Be a provider, not a hider.** So now that you have acknowledged the broader conversation—the good, the bad, and the ugly—and provided links to the information you want to highlight, you're done, right? Wrong. I would argue that you should go further: Put that information on your own site. If you only link to it, people leave your site and may never come back. They may even stay on a site that talks negatively about you. If you provide the good, bad, and ugly on your site, then three positive things can happen:

- First, once they get to your site, they won't feel the need to leave in order to get the other side's point of view. You get more time to engage them and tell your story. The more they linger, the more they wonder.

- Second, your message becomes more plausible because you acknowledge that the other side has their view as well. Rather than being the Sean Hannitys or Keith Olbermanns of the web, you become more of the Wikipedia, the place where people go to get a more complete sense of a topic.

- Third, when the information is being accessed through your site, you are the one who provides the context. You can provide perspective about how to look at the information and what you believe is most important.

Put simply, more information translates into more trust, even if, or perhaps because, some of the information goes against your point of view.

5. Always let other people comment on your site. Just as more information creates more trust, so does more openness. As you can imagine, many companies wrestle with the issue of whether to let the public comment on their sites. On the one hand, they want to engage the public, but on the other hand, they really only want the nice people to participate. Don't we all? Faced with the potential for strongly negative comments on their sites, they often opt to close the site entirely or provide only moderated comments in a futile attempt at keeping up appearances. Not too surprisingly, this is almost always a mistake. Here's why.

If you are a company with a great reputation like Ben & Jerry's, then you should allow comments because the frequency of negative ones is likely to be quite low. If you are on the other end of the spectrum and get a lot of hate mail as it is, like ExxonMobil, you should especially allow comments. Let's put it this way. No one over at ExxonMobil doesn't know they're a public enemy with more "haters" than you can shake a stick at. They know people are saying bad things about them. In fact, they're probably hard-pressed to find someone *not* saying bad things about them. The advantage of allowing comments on your website is that it's better to have them do it on your home turf where you can at least ensure a fair debate. Where the question of allowing comments gets a little more challenging is if you are a company or organization in the middle—one that isn't particularly hated or loved but just sort of treading water. Do you let people comment when it is possible that they will raise issues that no one else is paying attention to? Do you give credibility to your critics by giving them a podium when they don't really deserve to be listened to?

Ultimately, your job is to let the people decide who deserves credibility. If the question is whether consumers will be confused about which content to trust, user-generated or professional, the answer is *not* to make the decision for them. Instead, let them decide and self-police. Assuming you are responding rationally to the criticisms, your critics will start to look more and more irrational and you will look more and more credible. And when critics really push the boundaries, you will usually find that your own brand advocates will come to your defense. Because they are often more credible than you, it is a great position to be in when they start telling your side of the story for you.

Or you could shut down the comments and let people attack you from all over the rest of the web.

6. Be the voice of reason. Like being in a college-town bar around 1 a.m., there are plenty of screamers in the online world. The anonymity of the web seems to give everyone the ability to yell and scream in ways that they would never do in person. Fairly harmless incidents are reduced to expletive-laden tirades, while hyperbole is more the rule than the exception (for example, "This is the worst product in the history of the world. Ever."). Faced with lots of strongly worded criticism or commentary, many communicators naturally want to fight back, hard. The instinct is to mount an assertive, if not aggressive, defense. If you are an organization trying to build credibility with a skeptical audience, that instinct is probably wrong.

In the face of screamers, the best way to earn, or earn back, credibility is to be the voice of reason and moderation. Perhaps my favorite example of this is the "battle of the fact sheets" that often happens during a big issue or political campaign. Each side publishes its own fact sheet that uses extreme language to demonstrate the truth of its point of view. There is no room left for doubt. The next step is to publish a "myth vs. reality" document. This document is designed to rip apart the other side's fact sheet. It usually starts something like this: "The [other side's name here] is intentionally distorting the facts and misrepresenting the scientific findings of credible scientists. Instead of providing any real support for their gross accusations, this group relies on junk science to make its point. This document will uncover the myths about [other side's name's] claims and provide you with the truth about this issue." Each side typically publishes a document like this on its own site and then seeks to distribute it widely on the web.

The problem with this approach is that it too quickly reveals each side's agenda. More important, the forcefulness of the argument suggests that the company "doth protest too much" to be credible. Rather than settling the argument in the mind of the reader, the certainty and hyperbole of the argument do just the opposite— begging people to do another search to make sure that these are in fact the real facts, not some twisted version of them.

The much more effective approach is to be the voice of reason, to be the site and the speaker whose agenda is to help its customers or the public understand the issue so they can make the right choice. Together with transparency in showing the other side's argument and data, this rational approach gives readers greater confidence that they are getting an objective—and trustworthy—picture of the issue. And that they can stop looking for more information.

7. **Great customer engagement is the best way to build trust online.** This is going to be obvious to many, but it is still only standard business practice for a precious few companies. From the beginnings of the first Internet boom, Amazon.com understood that the Internet provided a unique and incredibly powerful way to engage with customers online. Companies like Netflix, Zipcar, and Zappos took online customer engagement to the next level. And now the explosion of apps for the iPhone is a further step in the direction of using the digital world to have a conversation with customers. These companies are there for customers when needed, where needed, and how needed. They recognize that the best way to get a new customer is to please one you already have. And so they work incredibly hard to make the customer experience a great one, thus making it a memorable one.

Talking to Your Customers When, Where, and How They Want You To

On Netflix it can seem like you receive an email confirmation that your movie has been received before you drop it in your mailbox. Netflix tells you when the next movie will arrive and what it will be. The company recognizes that the biggest problem with the online world is that people can't see the transaction taking place. We must place our trust in the seller to fulfill its half of the bargain. And when things take a little longer than we expect (which is often an unreasonably short period of time), we get anxious. Netflix makes sure that we never feel that anxiety.

Zipcar lets me know when my car needs to be returned so that I have enough time to make sure I am not late. Can you imagine Hertz doing that? Or the old Blockbuster calling you to ask you to return the movie you rented? Now Zipcar has a slightly different incentive because it has another customer waiting for the car, but it knows that communicating with me at the right time and in the right way is going to make my experience better and also improve the next customer's experience . . . even if Zipcar gets fewer late fees than it otherwise might.

It works for brick-and-mortar companies as well. In 2008, Starbucks launched MyStarbucksIdea to give customers a voice. It let people post ideas—good and bad, then it let them discuss and vote. The site then demonstrates that Starbucks is listening by letting users see the proof and explaining which ideas have been adopted and why.

The point is simple. The first rule of overcoming skepticism in a digital world is to use the tools at your disposal to communicate with customers when, where, and how your audience wants you to. There are few companies out there, from health insurers to retailers to e-commerce companies, that can't find better ways to build relationships and trust with their customers using digital tools and strategies.

In the end, the language of trust in an online world is not about changing your message to suit the medium. It's about understanding the medium so you can expand and maximize your message's reach and efficacy. All the rules outlined in the rest of this book still hold true. In fact, they are more true online because the skeptics in all of us have the opportunity to parse our words, check our facts, and look at what others are saying in an instant. The online world provides many more tools that we can use to tell our story, rebut the critics, and build credibility.

11

The Anti-Trust Laws:
Twenty Banned Phrases

Gary walked into a watch store one day with a friend who was looking seriously for a new and fairly expensive watch. The salesperson behind the counter spent a good hour with them showing different watches, asking questions, and building a strong rapport. From Gary's perspective, the salesperson had done a great job and would undoubtedly close the sale on that visit. Then, in what must have been a fit of impatience, the salesperson turned to Gary's friend and said, "Okay, so what will it take to get you to buy this watch today?" And in that moment, all the trust in the room disappeared. Gary and his friend walked out of the store.

If you ever watch *The Office*, you can relate to those phrases that come out of the characters' mouths that can only be referred to as "cringe-worthy." They are phrases so inappropriate to the circumstance or the times we live in that it is hard to listen to someone speak them.

In a world of skeptics, it is so hard to build trust and so easy to break it. In life and in communication, we are often judged by the single phrase in a long document or the single line in a sales pitch that caused the listener to turn off or tune out. While it is great to land on a phrase or sound bite that really resonates with your audience, it is often much easier to improve the effectiveness of your communication by getting rid of the language that hurts you. This chapter includes the biggest land mines we see along the path to building trust.

Many of these statements are well intentioned. In most cases, they are accurate and honest statements. But in a world of skeptics, they just don't make the grade.

Here are examples of twenty commonly used phrases that no longer inspire trust and now work against you.

"Are You Kidding Me?" Statements

These phrases are united by a common theme: it is hard to believe anyone would think that they can achieve their purpose.

1. **"Trust me" or "Trust us."** Yes, there are people and companies who still use this phrase. No, it doesn't work. People do not want to be told what to think. They certainly don't want to be told that they should abandon their well-ingrained skepticism with a simple phrase. If you need someone's trust, at least ask for it and give the audience a sense of what they will get in return: "We are committed to earning your trust and that is why we will do . . ." The corollary to this banned phrase is another set of words that should be banned: "honestly" or "frankly" or "to tell the truth." If one of your statements begins with "honestly," should I doubt all the others? We

have learned that when a politician or salesperson needs to talk about their own honesty, it is usually because they aren't.

2. **"If I could promise you this, would you buy . . ."** Much like the watch salesperson, this statement sounds like it belongs in a 1950s movie. It certainly doesn't work in today's environment. Statements like these reveal communicators that put their own interests well above their audience. They make it clear that the sale is what is important, not the needs or wants of the buyer.

3. **"We speak your language."** Really? If you did, would you need to tell me? Wouldn't it be fairly obvious? When you have a conversation with someone who speaks your language, do you tell them that you do so that they will realize? This is one of those phrases that suggests a company is just plain trying too hard. Chances are the next few statements will include some form of popular slang to further demonstrate the company's fluency. The bottom line: If you do speak your customer's language, speak it, don't talk about it. If you don't speak their language, telling them you do isn't going to make much difference.

Sincerely Unbelievable Statements

It is hard to convince many people that the companies that are responsible for customer service and communications actually do care about customers. It isn't in a purely unselfish way—these people do want to keep their jobs after all. But it is their job to try to improve customer satisfaction and help to ensure that customers stay customers. Unfortunately, some of the phrases that these communicators use to try to demonstrate their intentions have simply been overwhelmed by the reality of experiences that are entirely inconsistent with the words themselves.

4. **"Your call is important to us."** Presumably, that is why I am still on hold after five minutes and you won't let me hit 0 to get to a real human being. If your company has an automated system and your customers are going to be forced to sit and wait to talk to a live person, the message has to be better than this. It was the right sentiment and the right message when it was first used probably twenty years ago. Today, it is trite and inconsistent with the reality that people feel when they sit and wait and wait and wait to get their call answered. It is slightly better to tell people how long their wait will be. And better still to let them leave a number to get a return call at a specific time. But the companies that build trust are the ones that can demonstrate the call is important by actually picking up the phone.

5. **"We care about our customers."** I recently advised a company to stay away from this phrase and instead use the phrase, "Let us show you how we care." Why? Because skeptics generally reject as complete nonsense the idea that companies care about anything other than the bottom line. Say you care and people will give you a litany of examples of companies that said the same thing only to disappoint them. So rather than saying that you care, make a subtle but important shift by talking about how you will demonstrate that you care. Another phrase that should be banned for the same reason: "We take our responsibility seriously."

6. **"Our interests are aligned."** In one recent project, financial advisors tried to explain that their interests were aligned with their

clients. What did the clients say? If our interests are so aligned, why is it that when I make money, you make more, but when I lose money, you don't lose anything? In situations where interests truly are aligned, this is a great statement. But in most cases, this statement is just a poor attempt to get customers to believe that they are on the same side.

"Too Good to Be True" Statements

In the PTE, we are no longer willing to suspend our disbelief and believe just because you want us to. These statements are rejected because we don't believe in a free lunch and we don't believe in the basic truths suggested by these statements.

7. **"A best-of-breed product."** Quick—tell us how you would define the best automobile made. Would it have the fastest zero-to-sixty miles-per-hour acceleration? The highest reliability? The most exclusivity? The smoothest ride? Chances are that no two people would agree on the same definition, which is why no one car can ever claim the undisputed championship. This is why superlatives create doubt, not certainty, in the minds of others. If you have the best-of-breed product and so does your competitor, how do we know which one to buy? Are you both lying? Are you using different criteria? Either way, when most companies talk about themselves as the best in something (and most do), it dilutes the value of the claim. Today, it is virtually meaningless on its own. To make it credible, you must explain how you define "best," who declared you the best, and why it matters.

8. **"Achieving your dream retirement."** Only 12 percent of Americans believe that they can achieve a "dream retirement." (Even

before the financial crisis, only 15 percent believed it.) The rest feel it is an unrealistic, pie-in-the-sky construct, concocted by some ad writer. Images of tanned, fit senior citizens walking hand in hand along the beach may sound nice in theory, but they clash with the reality of how these investors really think. Even among the wealthiest 1 percent of the population, "maintaining their current lifestyle" ranks over a "dream retirement" by nearly three to one. So when financial services companies try to sell a dream retirement, it should be no surprise that their efforts fall flat.

9. **"We give you guaranteed results."** We spoke earlier in the book about how people no longer trust "guarantees," because too much has failed them in the past. Insurance companies failed to cover Hurricane Katrina victims. Lehman Brothers was considered "too big to fail" not long before its 2008 bankruptcy. And Bernie Madoff's clients believed that if they couldn't trust a former chairman of NASDAQ, who could they trust? As a result of these failures and many others, we reject the idea that anything in life can be truly guaranteed.

"Because I Said So" Statements

Some phrases today fail out of sheer arrogance. They are the kinds of things that your parents would say and cause you to roll your eyes. As a kid you might have to listen anyway, but as an adult you probably don't like the idea of someone telling you what to think.

10. **"Our products are safe."** In one research project we conducted to help an industry communicate about a product safety issue, the industry spokesperson liked to use this phrase because he

felt strongly that it was true. The problem was . . . the public didn't believe him at all. The more definitive his statement was, the less credible it became. Put simply, the public refused to believe what an industry spokesperson told them to believe. If this statement had come from the FDA, it would have been better but still subject to questions (we don't trust the FDA that much either). But coming from a corporate spokesperson the statement made it harder, rather than easier, to allay product safety concerns.

11. "This is the right product for you." Without a proper setup, lines like these are trust killers. For most people the reaction would be something like, "You don't know me, so how can you tell me what is right for me?" We see ourselves as unique individuals with specific needs—which means that we instinctively push back at anything that reduces us to a stereotype. Especially when it implies that you know more about selling to them than they do. Knowing the way your target market thinks is very important, but that never excuses you to start thinking about the person in front of you as a woman, a senior citizen, or a Latin American. If you do, they will push back and assert their individuality—and, in all likelihood, buy elsewhere. Too many salespeople try to tell prospects what to think about a product. Instead, the more effective approach is to give information, provide a perspective while recognizing it is only one side, and let the prospect draw the conclusion. If your product is what you say it is, then the prospects will make the right decisions. But if you try to force them to think a certain way, they will reject you for sport.

12. "The fact is . . ." One true "fact" out there today is that different people see the world in different ways. There are few facts about issues or products about which there is universally held agreement.

Gravity is a fact. The temperature at which water boils is a fact. But too often communicators believe they can rely on "facts" to make their argument. And too often the audience rejects the fact as telling only part of the story, or they counter it with another fact. In a world where we believe there is a statistic to support every argument, we can no longer rely on what we believe is incontrovertible fact to make our case or sell our product.

"When Worlds Collide" Statements

There are many situations where you are desperate to communicate your side of the story because, in your mind, you are in the right. You want the public or your customers to know as much as you do about the situation, and you feel that if you can just tell your story from your perspective you will win them over. Much of the time, your take on reality is not shared by your audience. They don't want to hear about your issues and they generally don't care what happens to your business. The following statements fail because they approach the world from your perspective rather than your audience's.

13. **"What you need to understand is . . ."** I have heard this statement too many times to count. Virtually every time it is followed by a statement that demonstrates that a salesperson or corporate communicator is losing a communication battle because they are trying to change their audience's worldview rather than accepting it and dealing with the consequences. As I tell my clients, "Your audience doesn't need to understand anything." They probably don't need to own your product or agree with you on a particular issue. So telling them that if only they could understand the "correct" point of view they would agree is an effort that usually fails.

14. "Our hands are tied." You've used this argument before. When you were six years old, and you tried to convince your parents that something was all Johnny's fault. And it didn't work very well then either. Today, companies try to explain that they were forced into situations by legal requirements or things outside of their control. GM did it before they went bankrupt. BP did it by initially trying to blame the oil rig owner for the explosion that caused the biggest oil spill in U.S. history. But even when it is true, trying to lay blame at someone else's doorstep rarely works. More often, you should accept ultimate responsibility to your customer or the public and then talk about how you will move forward and avoid a repeat of the experience.

15. "If we don't do this, it will hurt our business." There are many different forms of this statement as well, but the goal is always the same: to sell your audience an idea based on the notion that absent agreement with you, your business will suffer . . . and then so will the customer. We have seen utilities claim they will go bankrupt absent a rate increase. Pharma companies claim that importation of medications from Canada will kill medical innovation in the United States. And we have heard many companies claim that targeted taxes on their business will make it impossible to continue to operate. In virtually every case, we tell our clients the same thing: the public doesn't care about your problems. Unless you can frame the issue in a way that matters to them, your whining about the impact on your business will only erode trust.

"I Can Explain" Statements

Skeptics believe that you are guilty until proven innocent. So they are willing to accept a critic's portrayal of you as the bad guy without a great deal of circumspection. They also look for opportunities to place you into the stereotypical manipulative company frame. Here are three examples of statements that kill trust for these reasons.

16. **"This was taken out of context."** Not a shocker here, but if you have to communicate this statement, you are losing the communication battle. Unfortunately, your words can be manipulated to make you look bad. But we cannot identify an instance where making this statement on its own actually helps the situation. You have two choices in this situation. First, show the full statement and illustrate how someone else purposely manipulated your words. Or accept the statement and find something else to discuss. But using this statement as a defense is as effective as "no comment," which is to say, not effective at all.

17. **"I voted for the $87 billion before I voted against it."** This statement from John Kerry's 2004 presidential run is intended as a proxy for one of the surest trust killers out there: inconsistency. Getting the message right up front is so important today because as soon as you change your message, it will be thrown back in your face. And the mere fact that you have made a change is often perceived as an admission of guilt for the earlier statement. If you are caught in this situation, the best approach is to address the reasons behind your change of heart. The worst approach: trying to thread the needle and create some implausible explanation for why you weren't actually inconsistent (not coincidentally, this was the path John Kerry chose).

18. **Anything in fine print.** Show someone fine print in a brochure or a contract and they will point out that you are trying to hide something. In many cases, they will point to it as evidence of

an intent to deceive. And chances are they won't read it; they will just assume that it contains the provisions where the company takes advantage of the customer at its earliest possible opportunity. We tell our clients that fine print should be off-limits. It doesn't matter how long the document needs to become: fine print is killing your credibility. And if you must have fine print, you need to explain up front in large print why it is necessary to reduce the size of the print and where they can go to view it in full size.

Fearmongering Statements

19. **"Are you concerned about security for your family?"** And while we are at it, do you torture dogs and beat up old ladies? This is a loaded question that focuses solely on your selling interests because people know that if they answer yes, you will twist this answer around to why they need your product. The minute you ask it, the shields come up and your listener will be in full-scale defense mode. It also tries to use fear as an emotional driver for product consideration. But after nearly a century of hearing advertisers trying to scare us, and often exaggerating their case to do so, we have learned to shut down to fear-based selling. Speak in terms of opportunities, not risks. Burglar alarms can equate to safe homes, the right motor oil can translate to years of trouble-free performance, and a comfortable retirement often lies on the other side of a secure investment. Focus on what is most positive for your clients and customers, and then craft your message around it.

20. **"Act now or you'll miss this opportunity."** People love opportunities, but they hate artificially created fear. And in case you hadn't noticed, they had plenty of deadlines already before you came along

and decided to invent another one. One of the central tenets of sales and negotiating has been to create a sense of urgency. But we see something different in our own research nowadays: barging in with your own contrived sense of urgency destroys trust. It's okay to create short-term deals, promote them, and let people know they have a deadline. But unless you are their mother, don't lecture them on when they need to act.

Preventing Your Own Banned Phrases

This certainly isn't an exhaustive list of phrases that create mistrust, but it does represent the examples I hear most often in my work. Sometimes you can make these phrases work if placed in the appropriate context, but most of the time they are better avoided entirely. Unfortunately, there are plenty of other statements that do more harm than good and weren't even necessary to begin with.

If you go back over the phrases, you will see not only the themes that I have highlighted, but some broader themes as well.

The most significant is that banned phrases tend to be promises on which the communicator cannot deliver. They either overpromise or undersupport a claim.

Another theme is that they fit into the negative stereotypes that skeptics have created about companies and communicators who put their own interests before the customer.

And finally, banned phrases are often the ones that try to take control away from the audience rather than giving them information and putting them in control.

As you prepare your next pitch consider these final three themes. And see if you can avoid creating a new anti-trust law.

Epilogue: Building a New Age of Trust

Human beings have been communicating with each other for a long time—almost ten thousand years to be exact. During this time we have been through wars, cataclysms, economic catastrophes, and much more. So why has the language of trust suddenly become so important at the dawn of the twenty-first century?

The answer lies in a mix of factors unique to this point in history. First, we are more connected than ever. A generation ago or a thousand years ago, so-called experts told us things and we believed them. Today, *we* have become the experts, fueled by Google and social networks. When someone claims to have the best hotel, laundry detergent, or political platform, we are all a mouse click away from discovering that they don't.

Second, selling as we know it today is a fairly recent art. Sure, people have bought and sold since the dawn of time, and Jesus chased the money changers from the temple nearly two thousand years before consumer protection laws chased away the snake-oil salesmen. But the behavioral science of persuading people to buy things has a fairly recent history, much of which falls within our lifetimes.

Third and most important, we have had enough. We have seen too many promises turn into lies and spin, and too many salespeople whose answer to every question is to buy their product. We have watched institutions fail and businesses renege on their guarantees. Many of us have watched our hard-earned investments tumble in recent years. And after a while we've collectively said that enough is enough.

Meanwhile, we have learned more than ever about the psychology of how we communicate, how we make decisions, and how we trust each other. In the process we have learned the core lesson of this book: that selling products or ideas is dead, and building relationships of trust first is now the new way to sell. And looking to the longer term, it is clear that trust has now become the focal point for the future of how we communicate effectively with each other.

One of the greatest developments of human psychology in recent years has been cognitive-behavioral theory, which holds that the way we act springs from what we tell ourselves. It has formed the basis for powerful advances in treating mental illness by simply examining the language we use—for example, people are now often cured from fears or depression by gradually changing the false messages they send themselves.

Our own research shows that language is also an agent of social change on a much grander scale. We can see it already: when you hook up consumers to a dial testing session, the numbers show the difference between when trust is present or absent. It can be as subtle as the questions people now ask before making a purchase, or as dramatic as the closing of massive numbers of auto dealerships. Either way, society is learning the hard way that the era of talking people into things has come to an end.

This means that many of us will soon start using the language of trust in our daily communications. If we want to keep selling to or influencing others, we will have to. But this change, in turn, will have a social impact: we will start moving from a society that seeks to exploit others to one that seeks to inform and serve it. Success will come to those who become our most trusted resources, not those with the loudest voices.

This social change is not without its side effects. For example, how much spam do you get in your email inbox nowadays? You may see spam as a nuisance, but we see it as proof of a social trend: spammers with exaggerated sales pitches now have to send millions of emails to get just a few responses. And most of us filter it out and carry on with our lives. These spammers are like the canary in the coal mine, giving us a preview of the fate of hucksterism.

Another side effect is that when you now sell to anyone, you sell to everyone. How many people check product ratings on the Internet before they buy something these days? Almost everyone today relies on the wisdom of crowds in forming their buying opinions—whether it is a product, a service, or an election—and the humblest consumer now has a voice that is equal to your entire marketing department. This means that trust gained—or lost—now gets exposed to the sunshine of public opinion faster than ever.

Perhaps the most important side effect is how the words we use will help us emerge from an era of mistrust. A society that demands trust inevitably values honesty and authenticity, and this in turn channels our natural desires to sell and influence into a mandate to treat people with respect. We see the language of trust as not just a new way to succeed, but the cornerstone of a new era in what we say to each other.

It's All About You—and Me

This is a book about communications skills. But in a very real sense, it is one about a major change in society as well.

We have put forth a view of the world that is very different from even a generation ago. The four of us who wrote this book live in a country that was built on rugged individualism, competition, Darwinism, and an ethic of may the best man (or woman) win. Today, by comparison, we now live or die on the basis of interdependence. Our interests are linked, and so are our fates.

This means that we will no longer succeed unless we look at each other differently. The mentality of saying whatever is expedient, creating false urgency, making a sale or killing a piece of legislation at all costs, and scurrying back into our holes will eventually destroy us. We will get crushed under the weight of public opinion by a new public. And once we get kicked out, we may never be let back in.

On the other hand, we are now starting to embrace values that should have always mattered in the first place. Honesty. Transparency. Empathy. Acknowledgment. Traits that build long-term relationships. Traits that send out signals that people can trust you, and that it is safe to do business with you. But more important, traits that define us as human beings.

Will today's age of mistrust eventually lead us to a new generation of authentic communication? One that will perhaps stretch beyond the way we do business into better workplaces, political advocates, and personal relationships? And perhaps even usher in a new era of peace and global dialogue?

We believe that it will. And we believe that those of you who first start speaking the language of trust will become the leaders of this new era. We hope this book will help you succeed, but more important we hope it will help you evolve, at a time in history that we feel has limitless potential. Welcome to a brand-new world—one that is growing, as we speak, from the seeds of the words we use.

Endnotes

1 "Starr Report: Narrative." Nature of President Clinton's Relationship with Monica Lewinsky. Washington, DC: U.S. Government Printing Office, May 19, 2004, http://icreport.access.gpo.gov/report/6narrit.htm#N_1091. Citing Grand Jury Testimony of President William J. Clinton, August 17, 1998, at 59–61.

2 NAVA, "NAVA Reports Q3 2008 Variable Annuity Industry Data," December 12, 2008, www.navanet.org/pressroom/article/id/39.

3 Clay Shirky, "The Failure of #amazonfail," April 15, 2009, www.shirky.com/weblog/2009/04/the-failure-of-amazonfail.

4 Al Tompkins, "Monday Edition: Pain Reliever Warning," PoynterOnline (blog), August 29, 2004, http://poynteronline.org:80/dg.lts/id.2/aid.70592/column.htm.

5 Akio Toyoda, "Toyota's Plan to Repair Its Public Image," *Washington Post*, February 9, 2010, www.washingtonpost.com/wp-dyn/content/article/2010/02/08/AR2010020803078.html.

6 JetBlue, "An Apology from David Neeleman," www.jetblue.com/about/ourcompany/apology/index.html.

7 Conservation International, from "CI's Vision," www.conservation.org/discover/mission_strategy/pages/mission.aspx.

8 Kevin Cullen, "A Head with a Heart," *Boston Globe*, March 12, 2009; Paul Levy, "Running a Hospital," http://runningahospital.blogspot.com.

9 As president of MarketResearch.com in 1999, I was responsible for coming up with phrases like that to make our new site sound like it was both established and credible. We thought it worked back then but would not recommend that direction today.

10   P. C. Gordon, R. Hendrick, and W. H. Levine, "Memory-Load Interference in Syntactic Processing," *Psychological Science* 13 (5): September 2002.

11   Neil Postman, *Amusing Ourselves to Death: Public Discourse in the Age of Show Business.* New York: Penguin, 1985.

12   Michael D. Shear, "McCain Plans Fiercer Strategy Against Obama," *Washington Post,* October 4, 2008; W. H. Chang, J. Park, and S. W. Shim, "Effectiveness of Negative Political Advertising," *Web Journal of Mass Communication Research* 2 (1): December 1998, www.scripps.ohiou.edu/wjmcr/vol02/2-1a.htm.

13   Anastasia Meredith Oh, "Which Is Better, Coca-Cola or Pepsi?" Associated Content, August 26, 2008, www.associatedcontent.com/article/984476/which_is_better_coca_cola_or_pepsi.html?cat=35.

14   "Cut Out the Liver," *Time,* April 16, 1951; "Diet Pill Makers Fined Millions for False Claims," Associated Press, January 4, 2007.

15   Rudy Giuliani Television Ad "Tested," posted November 14, 2007, www.youtube.com/watch?v=FdjcF6hQ1O4&feature=channel.

16   American Psychological Association, "People Sometimes Seek the Truth, but Most Prefer Like-Minded Views," July 1, 2009, www.apa.org/news/press/releases/2009/07/like-minded.aspx.

17   The Pew Research Center for the People and the Press, "In general, would you describe your political views as . . . very conservative, conservative, moderate, liberal, or very liberal?" Conducted by Princeton Survey Research Associates International, February 4–8, 2009, and based on 1,303 telephone interviews, http://people-press.org/questions/?qid=1746970&pid=51&ccid=51#top.

18   The American Presidency Project, Second Bush–Dukakis Presidential Debate, October 13, 1988, Los Angeles, CA, www.presidency.ucsb.edu/showdebate.php?debateid=14.

19   Adele Westbrook and Oscar Ratti, *Aikido and the Dynamic Sphere.* Tokyo: Charles E. Tuttle Company, 1970, pp. 16–96.

20   Al Canata, "Chevron Says, 'Don't Buy Our Product,'" OpenMarket.org, October 24, 2008, www.openmarket.org/2008/10/24/chevron-says-dont-buy-our-product; Anheuser-Busch, "Corporate Social Responsibility," www.beeresponsible.com.

21   Luke 6:29, New American Standard Bible, Anaheim, CA: Foundation Publications, 1995.

22   The Perfect Apology, "Perfect Apology Business Cases," www.perfectapology
     .com/apology-business.html.

23   Todd Deferen, "Social Media on Main Street," PRsquared (blog), April 6,
     2009,   www.pr-squared.com/index.php/2009/04/social-media-on-main-street;
     Andy Beal, "Motrin Faces Twitter Headache over New Video Campaign,"
     Marketing Pilgrim (blog), November 16, 2008, www.marketingpilgrim
     .com/2008/11/motrin-faces-twitter-headache-over-new-video-campaign
     .html.

Index

About the Authors

Photo by Donna Watkins

Michael Maslansky is one of corporate America's leading communications and research strategists. As CEO of Maslansky, Luntz & Partners, he advises leading corporations, industry associations, major litigation practices, and nonprofit organizations on what to say, how to say it, and most important, why it matters. Michael's clients range from Fortune 500 firms such as PepsiCo, eBay, Pfizer, Starbucks, Bank of America, and Microsoft to associations for major industries such as health care, financial services, and biotechnology. He has conducted hundreds of research projects in more than twenty countries using his firm's trademarked polling and focus group methodology, lauded by the *New York Times*, *Washington Post*, *New Yorker*, *60 Minutes*, *Nightline*, and PBS's *Frontline*, among others. Michael is also a frequent commentator on CNN and has appeared on MSNBC, BBC World News, Al Jazeera, and other global media outlets.

Photo by Steven E. Gross

Scott West is managing director of marketing programs for Invesco. A nationally renowned speaker to the retail brokerage community, he is best known for creative marketing strategies geared to financial services professionals. He is the coauthor of *Story-selling for Financial Advisors* (Kaplan, 2000), *The Financial Professional's StoryBook* (Kaplan, 2004), and *Your Client's Story* (Kaplan, 2005).

Photo by Steven E. Gross

Gary DeMoss is managing director of Invesco, where he and his team provide communication and relationship skills to the financial services industry, and share processes, values, and personality approaches used by the masters in financial sales. Gary is a keynote speaker, seminar leader, and consultant to advisors who want to build their affluent client base, as well as an award-winning corporate sales and marketing executive. He is the coauthor of numerous books including *Making the Client Connection* (Kaplan, 2004), *Coaching the Sale* (Sourcebooks, 2006), and *The Top Performer's Guide to Attitude* (Sourcebooks, 2008).

Photo by Steven E. Gross

David Saylor is executive director of Invesco, in charge of creative development for the Invesco Van Kampen Consulting investment programs. He is best known for creating value-added marketing and presentations focused on baby boomers and senior investors, including their StorySelling, LanguAGEwave, and Finatical Curiosity programs. Over the past twenty years, his work experience has ranged from managing a trading desk, municipal underwriting, and retail brokerage, as well as managing the marketing communications for Invesco's $25 billion in fixed-income mutual funds. David is the coauthor of *The Financial Professional's StoryBook* with Scott West (Kaplan, 2004) and *Get Inspired to Retire* (Kaplan, 2006).